Babycare

Everything you need to know

Babycare

Everything you need to know

Ann Peters

DK

London • New York • Munich • Melbourne • Delhi

Project editor Claire Cross
Designer Hannah Moore
Senior editor Mandy Lebentz
Senior art editor Sarah Ponder
Managing editor Penny Warren
Managing art editor Glenda Fisher
Production editor Maria Elia
Production controller Alice Sykes
Creative technical support Sonia Charbonnier
Art director Lisa Lanzarini
Category publisher Peggy Vance
Editorial consultant Karen Sullivan
Photographer Ruth Jenkinson
Photography art direction Peggy Sadler

Every effort has been made to ensure that the information contained in this book is complete and accurate. However, neither the publisher nor the author are engaged in rendering professional advice or services to the individual reader. The ideas, procedures, and suggestions contained in the book are not intended as a substitute for consultation with your healthcare provider. All matters regarding the health of you and your child require medical supervision. Neither the publisher nor the author accept any legal responsibility for any personal injury or other damage or loss arising from the use or misuse of the information and advice in this book.

First published in Great Britain in 2011 by Dorling Kindersley Limited, 80 Strand, London, WC2R 0RL Penguin Group (UK)

2 4 6 8 10 9 7 5 3

006 – 178168 – Mar/11

A CIP catalogue of this book is available from the British Library

ISBN 978-1-4053-5816-3

Colour reproduction by Colourscan in Singapore
Printed in China

Discover more at
www.dk.com

Contents

Bonding with your baby

Stimulating your baby

Outings and lifestyle

About the author

Ann Peters RNHV has been a health visitor for over 20 years. Ann worked for the NHS for 19 years, where she managed a caseload of around 500 children at any one time, as well as establishing a sleep clinic and mothers' groups in Barnet. She retired from full-time NHS practice two years ago and has set up a successful private practice. She also works one day a week at a Family Centre, offering group work and health visiting support to parents and families. A mother of three and hands-on grandmother, she has also advised her husband, a GP and BMA Consulting Medical Editor, on a number of Dorling Kindersley health books.

Introduction

Every mother and father has their own unique story of parenthood, gained through their experience with their own child. Despite this personal experience, at some point most parents seek practical advice and reassurance from health professionals and experts, whether through direct contact, or from reading childcare manuals and websites. When I gave birth to my twins, I realized that, even as an experienced health visitor, there was a lot of learning to be done, and I sought advice from others, too. The advice offered by the different childcare experts of the day was often conflicting, with some advocating leaving babies to cry, while others stressed the importance of attending to babies' needs. Today, this conflict of advice remains, and can be even more confusing with all the information available.

This book aims to set out a path through the conflicting advice, providing parents with clear, easy-to-follow guidelines on the important areas of everyday care, feeding and sleeping. The chapters are set out in a logical order, with information on feeding preceding sleep, the idea being that when feeding goes well, then babies sleep more easily and soundly. Later chapters offer valuable advice on adjusting to family life, bonding with your baby and enhancing your baby's development, as well as looking at the practicalities of travel and outings with your baby. The book concludes with advice for mothers planning a return to work and tips on achieving a work-life balance. All the information is based on sound evidence and practical experience. The many mothers I have had the privilege to work with have been a huge source of knowledge and inspiration, and we have incorporated this into the book.

I have worked closely with the team at DK – all mothers with different views and experiences – and together we have pooled our knowledge to create this book: an invaluable guide to babycare in the first year of life.

Ann Peters

Ann Peters

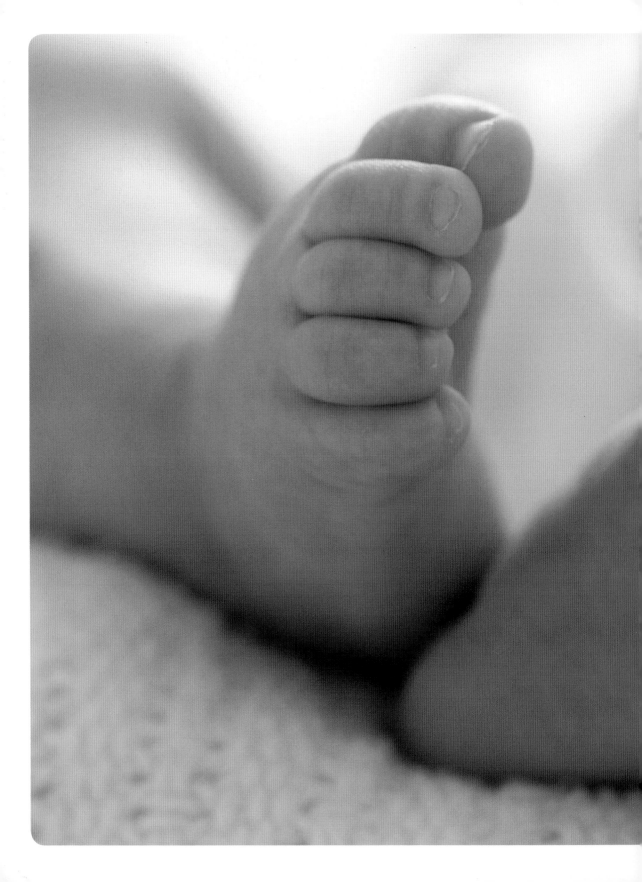

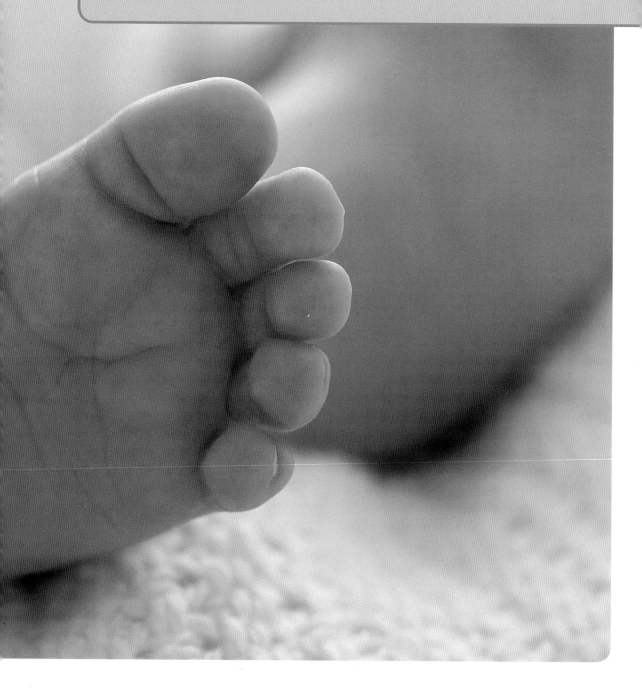

Caring for your baby

GETTING STARTED

Your new baby will have her own temperament, personality and needs, and it can take a little while to get to know her. Rest assured, though, that over time you will learn to understand her needs and handle her capably and confidently.

IS YOUR BABY COMFORTABLE? One of the most important things to consider when caring for your new baby is her comfort. Making sure that your baby has a full tummy, clean nappy, appropriately warm clothing and bedding, and the stimulation, love and affection she needs will keep her content, and able to grow, develop and explore the world around her without distraction. All babies have different needs, and you'll discover these as you get to know your new baby. However, the things you do on a day-to-day basis – making sure your baby is well fed, winded, held comfortably, bathed regularly, getting plenty of sleep, and even wearing clothes that fit her – will make the job of keeping her comfortable and happy that much easier. Comfortable babies are happy babies.

SAFETY FIRST Keeping your baby healthy and happy is undoubtedly your main concern, and it goes without saying that you, like all parents, want the very best for your new arrival. Your love will shine through in everything you do for your baby, even when you feel tired and frustrated; try to remember that your baby will sense this, and become that much more content as a result. It is, however, equally important to remember that your baby's safety must be a top priority. The way you handle her, set up her environment, bathe and dress her, and even entertain her, must be undertaken with scrupulous attention to her safety. Protecting her from the potential pitfalls in daily life will not only help you to become a more confident parent, but also help your baby feel relaxed and secure. Throughout this chapter, you'll learn the best ways to keep your baby safe while you go about her everyday care.

BABY BASICS Getting to grips with the basics can make the job of caring for your baby easier, as you relax into parenthood, confident of your ability to get things done. All babies are different, and no technique will always work, but if you have a clear idea of the best way to go about bathing and changing her, looking after her teeth and skin, and caring for her when she is ill, the job of looking after your baby will run that much more smoothly.

Above all, trust your instincts: try not to panic when things don't go exactly to plan, or you are unsure about your abilities as a parent. If your baby is loved and cared for, she'll be just fine.

GETTING ORGANIZED No two days are ever the same when you have a baby in the house, and just when you think you've got new parenthood cracked, your baby will adjust her routine or make unanticipated demands on your time and energy.

Taking the time to organise yourself and your baby's belongings can make a huge difference to how you feel and manage. In fact, a few moments spent topping up your changing bag, setting out your baby's towel and sleepsuit in advance of her bath, and ensuring that you have some warm water ready when it's time to change her nappy, can help you to keep on top of her daily care, and enable you to relax and enjoy being a new parent.

Close contact Interacting with your baby through touch, words and looks, helps you get to know her and be alert to her needs.

Your baby's comfort A clean nappy, full tummy and comfortable environment will all help to keep your baby content.

ENJOY! If you were highly organised, tidy, busy and ambitious before the birth of your baby, you may struggle with the idea that

now your house is a mess, the fridge is empty, your to-do list is growing rather than acquiring neat little ticks, and you seem to do nothing more than change, feed and soothe your baby for hours and hours on end – but stop right there. It may be hard to believe right now, but your baby will grow and develop quickly, and it's important to savour every moment along the way.

No matter what you did before, or how you organised your life, remind yourself that your new job is caring for your baby, and that involves keeping her safe, comfortable and happy, no matter how long it takes.

Try to take the pressure off yourself, and lower your expectations of what you need to achieve each day. Keep your to-do list short, and simply concentrate on the thing that matters most – caring for your new baby. A healthy, happy baby is worth far more than a dust-free home and perfectly ironed pillowcases. Take the time to immerse yourself in motherhood, and enjoy the little things: snuggle up and relish feeding your baby and enjoy her adoring gaze and sweet-smelling warmth.

Everyday care As you get to grips with the basics of babycare, you'll become a more confident parent, and your baby will feel reassured as he will know what to expect.

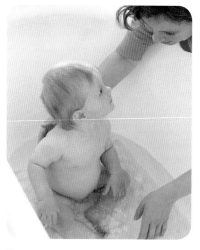

Your baby's safety One of your priorities is your baby's safety, and your vigilance is essential to be sure of this.

Being prepared Once you have a baby, you'll soon realise that being organized will help your days to run smoothly.

Picking up your baby

Your new baby will seem impossibly small and fragile, and you may feel nervous about picking him up – and even dropping him. By following these simple steps you will keep him safe and help make him feel secure.

Holding your young baby

There are a number of different ways to hold your newborn baby safely. As you gain confidence, you'll enjoy finding positions in which you both feel comfortable and your baby is content.

★ Many parents naturally use the cradle hold when their baby is very young, which means cradling your baby in your arms, as shown right. Most babies love this position because they can see you, and their body is close to yours. This position also supports your baby's neck, which is important in the early days before he gains muscle strength.

★ You can rest your young baby against your shoulder. Use the hand that is not supporting his bottom to keep his back and head against you. This is a great position for winding, and also helps your baby drift off to sleep. Many babies like to have their bottoms patted while being held, probably because mums unconsciously pat their tummies when they are pregnant.

★ As you gain more confidence, you can hold your baby face down in your arms so that his head rests on your forearm and your hands support his tummy and legs (see opposite).

1 **To pick up your newborn baby securely**, start by sliding one of your hands underneath your baby's head. Your hand should cover part of his neck as well as his head.

2 **Take your other hand** and slide it underneath your baby's bottom. Both of your hands should now be underneath your baby, supporting both his head and his bottom as you lift him.

3 **Gently lift your baby** towards your chest. Slide the hand behind his head around his body to cradle him. Pull him close to your chest and support his head and neck in the crook of your elbow.

4 **Always support your baby's head** so that it doesn't fall back or roll forwards. His neck muscles take time to develop, but he'll gradually be able to hold his head upright and look around.

Carrying your newborn in a sling

Many parents enjoy using a sling (see p.172) to carry their newborn baby – both indoors and for trips out.

Keeping your baby safe Choose a brand and a style that allows your baby to move his arms, and which keeps him in an upright position, so that his breathing isn't restricted.

Hands free Slings allow you to get on with other things around the home, while still staying in close contact with your baby. Many fractious babies will be soothed off to sleep by both the closeness of your body, and the movement. It's important to be careful, though: don't lean over the cooker, or anything hot, and take care when bending over that there's nothing that can hit your baby's head.

Easy access Choose a sling that opens easily for changing. Some have detachable "bodies", so that you can get your baby out while the straps remain in place.

Face down Your baby may be comfortable resting upon your forearm, with his head on your arm and your hands supporting his bottom and legs. This is a good position for winding as gravity helps with the release of trapped air.

Lifting your older baby

As your baby grows, she may have her own ideas about how and when she should be picked up. You'll need to find ways to pick her up and hold her that keep her safe and secure and don't put you under strain.

1 **Bend your knees** and keep your back straight to avoid straining it. Reach out and, from a crouching position, hold your baby firmly under her arms and gently lift her.

TOP TIP
Use words and gestures as you pick up your baby. Say "ups-a-daisy" in a sing-song voice as you reach out. She'll start to recognize what is happening and lift up her arms in anticipation.

2 **As you rise**, use your leg muscles to provide leverage, and keep your back straight. Bring your baby up to your body, rather than your body to your baby.

Facing the world As your baby becomes older and requires less support to her back, neck and head, she'll love facing outwards and seeing everything that you see. Always hold her carefully, with a firm grip on one thigh and your arm around her chest.

Watching your back While it's very convenient to hold your baby on one hip, it can cause back problems. If you do hold her in this way, change hips from time to time and keep one arm firmly around her bottom and legs.

On the move Your growing baby will enjoy being held in different positions, and experimenting with her body. Holding her firmly under her arms and bottom, you can "fly" her around the room and point out all sorts of things that may interest her.

Up high Everything you do with your baby teaches her something about the world around her, so give her a bird's-eye view. Raise her in the air and swing her up and down. She'll find it an amusing game and you can enjoy her giggles.

Safe handling

Follow these guidelines to be sure that you're holding your baby securely while keeping an eye on your posture, too.

★ **The ideal way to hold your baby** is in an upright position, directly against your chest, in the centre. When she's a little older, she will be able to latch her legs around you, but until then, support her bottom with one arm, and hold her upper back with the other.

★ **While holding your older baby on a hip** can be a great way to free up a hand (see left), take care not to do so for more than a few minutes. Over time, you can develop postural imbalances that can cause lower back pain. Hip-holds free up one of your arms to do other things, but be careful when bending, and always keep a firm grip on your baby.

★ **As your baby's confidence grows**, and her muscles and coordination develop, your baby will begin to wriggle – with excitement, to reach out and grab something, or because she suddenly decides that she wants to get down. Be prepared for sudden shifts – not only is it possible to drop her, but you could hurt your back trying to keep her upright. Keep a firm hand on at least one leg at all times.

★ **When you lie your baby down** in her cot when she is dozing, hold your hand under her head as you did when she was a newborn: she has little control over her head and neck when asleep. Bend your knees and keep your back straight as you put her down.

Using nappies

Not all babies enjoy having their nappy changed, but being organised and having everything to hand will make changing time easier for both of you.

Disposable nappies These are convenient and easy to use but they are not very environmentally friendly. They are very absorbent: most contain a moisture-retaining gel, which soaks up urine so that the layer next to your baby's skin stays dry.

Reusable nappies Fabric nappies these days are as easy to use as disposables, less expensive in the long run (you can also use them for a second child), and they also create far less waste. You'll need nappy liners and overpants (see p.19).

Your changing bag Keep this stocked and ready to go. As well as a travel mat, nappies, wipes and clean baby clothes, you may want to include breast pads, nipple cream, water and snacks for you. If you're bottlefeeding, pack a box of formula and a sterilized bottle.

Changing mats A wipe-clean, padded mat is an essential part of your nappy-changing equipment. Keep a foldaway mat in your travel bag. Some have a wipe-clean surface on one side and towelling on the other, so act as impromptu play mats when you're out.

Cleaning equipment A water spray and a thin flannel are best for cleaning bottoms. Wipes are convenient, but harsh, so shouldn't be used for the first six weeks. If you use cotton wool, make sure that you don't leave any strands in creases or around the penis.

Barrier cream This protects your baby's bottom from the effects of urine and faeces, and can also soothe nappy rash. It isn't necessary all the time, but it's worth having in the event that his bottom becomes sore. Keep a travel tube in your changing bag.

Changing units A changing station with drawers or shelves is a good place to keep nappies, wipes and all the nappy-changing paraphernalia you need so that it's all to hand. Most units have raised edges to help prevent a baby from rolling off but never leave a baby unattended even for a second. Choose a unit at waist-height to protect your back.

Disposables and reusables

The jury is still out about the environmental benefits of reusable nappies, but it does seem that they're around 10 percent greener, and most definitely less expensive over time.

Reusable nappies These come in a range of colours and styles, and apart from the initial outlay, are more economical. They produce less waste, use fewer raw materials in their manufacture and your baby will have soft, natural fibres next to his skin. However, washing reusables can produce a great deal of waste water, uses cleansing agents and chemicals and can be time-consuming too, unless you can afford a laundry service. Your baby will need to be changed more often, as reusables tend to be less absorbent. They can take a long time to dry, and using a tumble-dryer has an environmental impact. You'll need 15–20 plus accessories, such as liners, plastic overpants and storage buckets, and you will have to transport wet and soiled nappies when you're away from home.

Disposable nappies These are more convenient and many are now biodegradable and chemical free, making them kinder to the environment – and your baby's skin. There also appear to be fewer cases of nappy rash, fewer leaks and fewer changes necessary. They are, though, more expensive, produce a high level of waste, and must be disposed of properly. The majority contain man-made chemicals, too.

Changing a reusable nappy

Forget the pins and folding: reusable nappies have moved on, and are now made from lightweight materials that are easy to wash and dry and come with easy-to-use fastenings and poppers.

What you'll need

Organize the following before you begin:

★ A warm area with a clean changing mat or towel for your baby to lie on

★ A clean, dry nappy

★ A nappy liner

★ A plastic or rubber wrap, or overpants unless you choose an all-in-one nappy, (see opposite)

★ Nappy pins or clips, or plastic nappy grips, if you choose pre-folded or towelling nappies

★ Warm water, a thin flannel or cotton wool or baby wipes to clean her bottom

★ Barrier cream to prevent nappy rash

★ A large bucket to store soiled nappies before washing

★ A plastic bag to transport the soiled nappy home if you're out and about

TOP TIP
You'll need to buy 15–20 reusable nappies, which allows you to wash every other day when your baby is small, plus 3–4 waterproof overpants or wraps.

1 **Unfasten the wrap and the nappy.** Fold the nappy in half under your baby, with the unsoiled side up, taking care to wipe away any faeces with the nappy. Remove the soiled nappy.

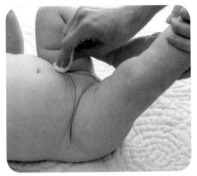

2 **Use warm water** with a thin, clean flannel or cotton wool to wash your baby from front to back thoroughly. Sing or chat to her as you do, so she'll associate nappy changes with pleasure.

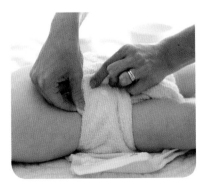

3 **Lay the clean nappy on a wrap** with a nappy liner on top. Slide it under your baby, and apply a little barrier cream. Fasten the nappy, pinching the fabric between the legs to avoid bunching.

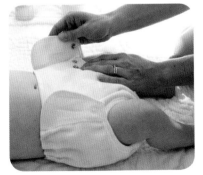

4 **Secure the wrap**, making sure that it's fastened firmly. Run your fingers over the edge to check it covers the nappy. The waist should be snug without pinching the skin. Wash your hands.

Buying reusable nappies

There is a wide range of reusable nappies on the market to fit your individual needs and budget. They fall roughly into two types:

Two-part nappies These consist of a nappy and an outer wrap. Nappies can be traditional towelling, which will require pins or clips, a folded nappy (known as a pre-fold and which also requires a fastener) or a shaped nappy. Over the top of the nappy, you will place a wrap designed to keep the moisture in and prevent the nappy from leaking. Wraps can take the form of a pull-up pair of pants, or may be wrap-around with fastenings that are often Velcro. You won't need to use new overpants with every change – only if they are soiled or very wet.

All-in-one nappies These combine the inner nappy and the outer wrap in a single waterproof garment. These nappies look a little more like disposables, and they are normally self-fastening, avoiding the need for fastening pins or clips. Some parents find them harder to wash and dry thoroughly because they are bulkier. They also tend to leak more than the two-part nappies.

Disposable nappy liners These provide a barrier between the fabric and your baby's skin, and they also make it easier to lift out and dispose of faeces. Biodegradeable nappy liners are available. Booster pads can be useful during the night as they provide greater absorbency.

Changing a disposable nappy

Many parents find it easier to use disposables when they're out and about, and at night, because of their added absorbency. Choose the most appropriate nappy for your baby's size so that it fits him neatly.

What you'll need

Make sure you have the following items before changing a nappy:

★ A warm area with a clean changing mat or towel for your baby to lie on

★ A clean nappy

★ Warm water and a thin flannel or cotton wool or baby wipes to clean his bottom

★ A plastic bag/nappy bin for disposal

★ Barrier cream if your baby is prone to nappy rash

1 **Place your baby on a clean surface** and remove the soiled nappy. Clean the nappy area (see p.22). Lift his legs and place a clean nappy under his bottom, with the tabs under his waist.

2 **Gently bring the nappy up** between his legs. For boy babies makes sure the penis is tucked down as you pull up the front of the nappy. Fold over the fastening sides securely.

3 **Ensure that the nappy doesn't gather** between the legs. Fasten firmly, so that the nappy feels snug, but not too tight. You should be able to fit your finger between the tummy and nappy.

4 **Put your baby in a safe place** before you turn or move away to place the used nappy either in a nappy bin or in a nappy bag for disposal. Wash your hands thoroughly.

TOP TIP
Buying disposable nappies in bulk can be cheaper. If you shop online, you can get them delivered too. Compare supermarket prices and look out for money-off coupons.

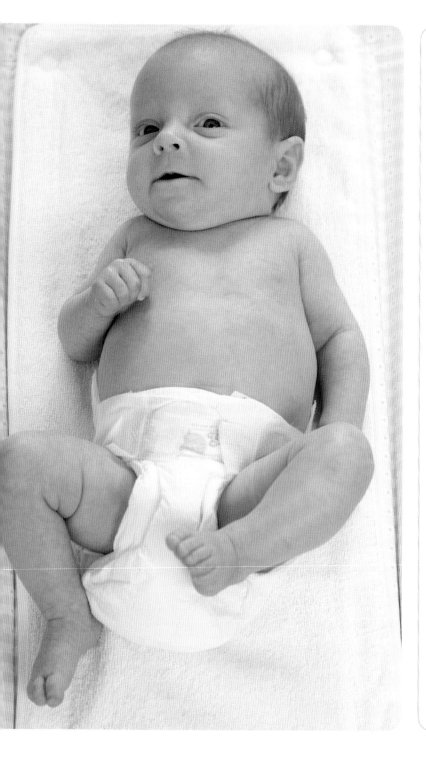

Your baby's nappy contents

Being aware of what's normal and what's not when it comes to the contents of your baby's nappies can save unnecessary worrying.

Wet nappies Most babies have between six and eight wet nappies each day (with newborns having up to 12 wet nappies a day). Hydrated babies produce pale yellow urine and soft stools. If his urine is dark yellow or smelly, he may not be feeding well or may have an infection. Babies can easily become dehydrated, so see your doctor or health visitor if he has fewer wet nappies than usual.

Bowel movements These vary according to your baby's age and whether you're breastfeeding. For the first few days, babies pass meconium, a thick, dark-green or black substance that was in his intestines before birth. Breastfed babies then often have liquid, mustard-yellow or yellowish-green movements. Little lumps, like milk curds, are also normal. The frequency of breastfed babies' bowel movements varies. Bottle-fed babies bowel movements are usually daily and often thicker, pasty and smellier.

Bowel movements do vary from baby to baby. As long as your baby's stools are not dry and hard (which can indicate constipation), there is nothing to worry about. When solid food is added to your baby's diet, his stools become firmer and brownish.

When to be concerned If your baby's bowel movements change, or you see blood or mucus in his stools, see your doctor to rule out problems.

Cleaning your baby's bottom

Keeping your baby's bottom clean not only helps to prevent nappy rash, but also discourages the build-up of organisms that can lead to infection. Pay particular attention to the little creases and folds of her body.

What you need to know

Follow these guidelines to keep your baby's bottom clean and rash-free.

★ Change your baby's nappy regularly, about every two to three hours. Newborns tend to need their nappies changed more often than older babies – about every one to two hours in the day. Older babies and toddlers can usually go a little longer, but may be changed every two to four hours.

★ Change your baby's nappy as soon as possible after a bowel movement.

★ Reusable nappies tend to be less absorbent than disposables, and you may need to change them more often.

★ If your baby has a nappy rash, more frequent changes may be required. It can help to leave her without a nappy for short periods of time to help her skin dry and heal.

★ Avoid using scented nappy wipes that can irritate your baby's skin. Look for hypoallergenic wipes or use warm water and a flannel or cotton wool instead.

★ Always hold your baby firmly with one arm – rolling is a trick that babies appear to learn at any age. Some parents like to hold a clean nappy over the penis while they clean their baby boy to avoid an unexpected shower!

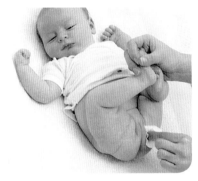

1 **Always clean your baby girl's bottom** from front to back to help prevent urinary tract infections. Gently wash the skin folds of her thighs and around her genitals.

2 **Clean down her genitals** to her buttocks, then lift her legs to clean her lower back. Don't clean in the creases of her vagina as she has an effective self-cleaning mechanism here.

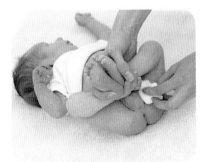

1 **Lift up your baby boy's penis** and clean underneath, and then down and under his scrotum. Always clean his penis gently, and don't be tempted to pull back the foreskin.

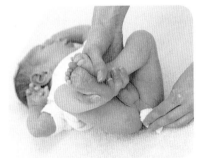

2 **Once you've cleaned** around your baby's penis and scrotum, clean down around his bottom, paying particular attention to the crease of his buttocks and the folds of his thighs.

Preventing nappy rash

Nappy rash is caused by contact with urine or faeces, which cause the skin to produce less protective oil and therefore provide a less effective barrier to further irritation. Almost all babies suffer from uncomfortable nappy rash at some point. Here are the best ways to deal with it.

Frequent changes No matter how absorbent your baby's nappy, moisture will always get through, so change him often to keep him as clean and dry as possible and protect his delicate skin against irritation.

Nappy-free time Put your baby on his mat in a safe place, such as on the floor, and take his nappy off for a while so that air can circulate around his skin. You may want to lay a towel on the mat in case of accidents.

Soothing nappy rash

Follow the tips below to help soothe any soreness and keep nappy rash at bay:

★ If you're using reusable nappies, consider changing to disposable nappies for a short time because they are more absorbent so tend to be better at keeping urine away from the skin.

★ If you continue to use reusables, put them through an extra rinse cycle to be sure you have eliminated any traces of detergent.

★ Zinc oxide is an excellent barrier cream for the nappy area, and can also encourage healing.

★ If your baby's nappy rash has white patches, he may have thrush; antifungal ointments can be prescribed. In severe cases, your doctor may recommend a mild hydrocortisone ointment or cream.

★ Avoid using soap or other detergents on the nappy area. Rinse carefully with clean water at each nappy change.

★ Ensure your baby is drinking enough, as this reduces the acidity of his urine.

★ Any nappy rash that does not heal with treatments within a week or so should be seen by a doctor.

★ If the rash becomes infected, seek medical help straightaway to clear the infection and stop it spreading.

Protecting your baby's bottom Apply a thin layer of barrier cream to your baby's bottom; use your finger to smooth it into the folds and crevices. If his bottom is sore, leave his nappy off for a little while before applying the cream.

Topping and tailing

Newborns don't need a daily bath, and at first bathing can be a stressful experience for both babies and parents. In the early weeks, topping and tailing with a sponge or a thin flannel and some cotton wool in between baths is fine. Make sure you have everything to hand before you begin.

What you'll need

Gather together the following before you start to wash your baby:

★ A bowl or basin of warm water

★ Mild hypoallergenic baby wash, if desired

★ Cotton wool or pads, or a sponge or thin flannel

★ A towel

★ A clean nappy

★ Nappy cream, if desired

1 **Wash your hands**. To clean your baby's eyes, use cooled boiled water and a clean cotton pad for each eye to avoid transferring infection. Gently wipe from the inside to the outer edge.

2 **Fill a sink or basin with warm water** – if you wish, add a few drops of baby bath or wash. Dampen a flannel or cotton wool and gently clean her face, behind her ears and in the neck creases.

TOP TIP
If your baby has a dirty nappy, wash her back and bottom last. Leaving her nappy on until the end avoids little accidents when cleaning other parts!

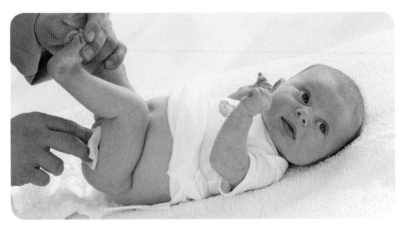

3 **Lay your baby on a safe surface**, preferably near to a sink and, using a sponge, flannel or cotton wool, gently wash under her arms, across her tummy, and around her genital area. If your baby's bottom is dirty, clean this area first and change the water before cleaning elsewhere.

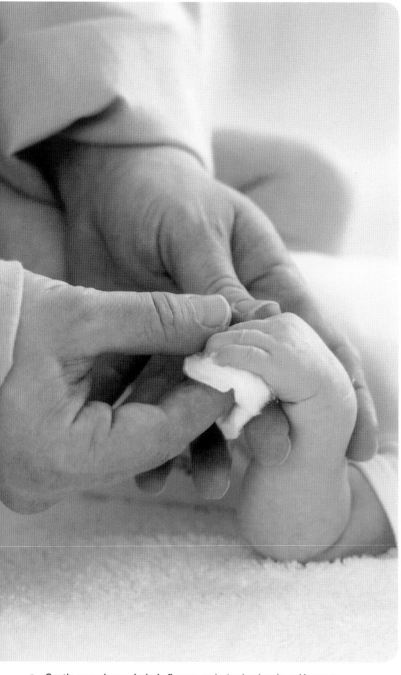

Gently uncurl your baby's fingers and wipe her hands and between her fingers with the flannel or a new piece of cotton wool. Finally, pat her hands and fingers dry with a towel.

Toiletries and skin care

You won't need much to keep your baby clean and fresh-smelling and to prevent her skin from drying, but it is worth investing in a few good-quality products to make the job easier.

Baby wash and shampoo It's a good idea to choose a combined product, which saves both money and time. Natural baby products are the best choices because they are guaranteed to contain no chemicals that could harm your baby or cause irritation to her tender skin or eyes.

Caring for dry skin If your baby's skin is dry, you may wish to purchase an emollient baby lotion. Again, natural products are best. Always choose a fragrance-free brand designed for young babies, which will be gentle enough to see her through the first year of life. However, avoid using baby lotion on newborns and very young infants as their skin is still immature.

Many parents now choose to add just a little olive oil to their baby's bath, instead of using toiletries. This natural alternative helps to keep her skin hydrated, and is free from any chemical irritants.

Barrier creams (see p.23) These are an essential, as almost all babies will benefit from having a little applied to their bottoms between nappy changes. Brands containing zinc oxide are best for soothing irritated skin and providing a barrier against urine and faeces.

Cleaning creases

Your baby's skin has lots of little creases and folds where dirt can become trapped and irritate his delicate skin over time. Clean these regularly to prevent any soreness.

Taking care

It's important to pay attention to the skin folds when cleaning your baby, as the skin here can become damp and irritated.

★ To clean your baby's creases, wet a thin flannel or some cotton wool with warm water and, if desired, a drop of baby wash. If using a flannel, wring this dry, and clean under and around the skin creases. If you use cotton wool, take care not to leave any threads or fluff behind, as they can cause irritation.

★ Clean behind the knees, under his chin, around his neck (where folds can trap spilt milk and possetting), under his arms, in between his fingers and toes, and around his genitals and thighs.

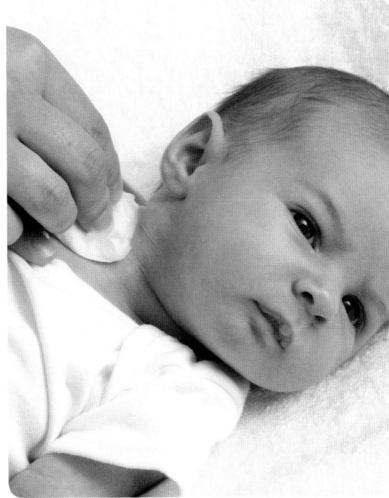

Under the arms Gently lift your baby's arms and hold his hand in yours while you use your other hand to clean carefully in the creases of the skin under and around your baby's armpits.

Cleaning the neck Pay attention to the folds in your baby's neck: use a wet flannel or cotton wool to clean in the creases and remove any fluff or dirt. For stubborn accumulations, moisten your finger with a little olive oil and run it through the creases and folds, which soothes the skin as you clean.

Caring for your baby's umbilical cord stump

The stump of your baby's umbilical cord will usually dry, blacken and drop off between five and 15 days after her birth. A small wound or sore will remain, but this should heal within a few days.

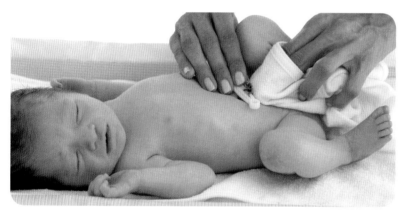

Careful cleaning It was once advised that alcohol and an antiseptic be used on the umbilical stump; however, now it's recommended that plain water is used. If the cord area is soiled, use soapy water to remove any faeces.

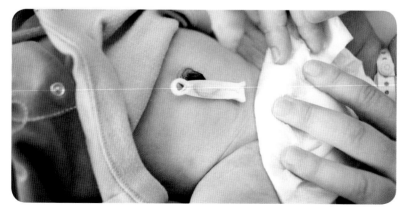

Helping it heal Look for "bikini" nappies, cut below the belly button, which allow the stump to dry. Or turn down the nappy to leave the stump open to the air, and prevent urine and faeces coming into contact with it.

Umbilical care tips

Follow some simple guidelines to ensure good care of your baby's cord area.

★ **Always wash your hands** carefully before cleaning around your baby's cord.

★ It's fine to give your baby a full bath with the stump still attached.

★ **Avoid soap products** unless the area has become very dirty. However, if there is faeces around the cord area, use a mild soap, as the fatty deposits in stools are harder to remove with plain water.

★ If the site becomes red or inflamed, or there's a smelly discharge, see your doctor or midwife to rule out an infection.

★ After the stump falls off, it takes seven to 10 days to heal completely. It's normal to see a little blood on your baby's nappy when the stump drops off, so don't be alarmed by this.

KEY FACT

It's usual for the cord stump to look a little mucky, and to have a yellowish discharge at the base. The stump will eventually drop off and the area will heal fully.

Bathtime equipment

Most babies love bathtime: once it becomes a part of their routine they find the warm water soothing, and grow to enjoy this special time with mum or dad. Help bathtimes run smoothly by preparing everything in advance and ensuring that the water is the correct temperature.

Baby baths These are a good investment if your kitchen sink is in constant use, or your bathroom basin is too small. Some parents put the bath inside the main bath. Run the cold water first: it's safer to top up with hot water than to cool down a too-hot bath.

Flannels and sponges Baby-sized flannels make getting into little crevices easier, but a normal flannel or a natural sponge will do just as well. Many babies like to play with sponges, and giving them a good squeeze over your baby's head will rinse his hair.

Shampoos and washes Use these sparingly as your baby doesn't need lots of products to keep clean. A combined baby wash and shampoo is ideal, or add a little olive oil to the bath. Special jugs help to stop water going in the eyes during hair washing.

Bath seats These can be used once your baby can sit unaided. A seat means he can play independently, and your hands are free to wash him. Don't assume that he's safe, though: he will still need supervision.

Bath thermometers These indicate when your baby's bath water is the ideal temperature (35–38°C/95–100°F). Many simply change colour when the temperature is right, and some double up as bath toys.

Bath mats Use a non-slip mat in the bath: both baths and babies are slippery when wet. A bath mat is essential once he sits up as it's easy for him to slip. Keep a hand on your baby's arm or leg at all times.

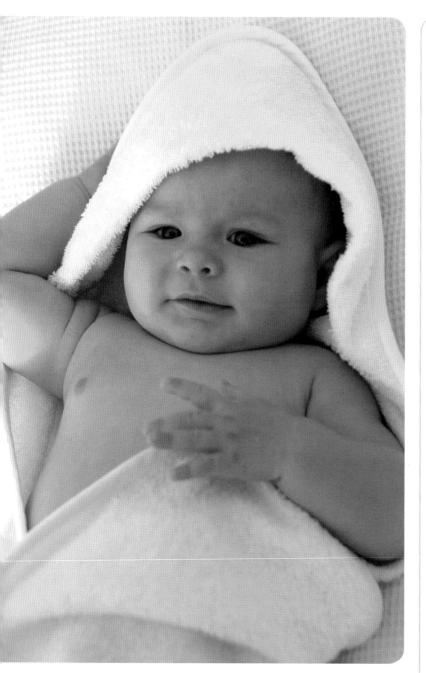

Dry and snug Dry your baby carefully after the bath, particularly in his creases and folds. A hooded towel is ideal for young babies, who tend to lose heat quickly. Pop the hood over his head, and use the towel base to dry the rest of his body carefully.

Bathtime basics

Following simple guidelines keeps your baby safe and happy during bathtime.

The right temperature Use your elbow or forearm to test the water temperature, which should be just warm to the touch. If in doubt, you can invest in a bath thermometer (see left). Always run a little cold water through a mixer tap after running your baby's bath to prevent any drips – or the tap itself – from burning him.

Constant supervision Always hold your baby carefully when bathing him, and never leave him unattended, even for a few seconds. Placing your forearm behind his head and neck and gently holding your baby's upper arm will keep him safe.

Keep your baby warm Young babies lose body heat quickly, so don't undress him until the bath is ready and have a warm, dry towel ready for as soon as you remove him.

Bath toys These are a good distraction for older, sitting babies, especially ones who are reluctant to bathe. Choose some that bob in the water, or pour water when lifted.

Baby baths If you use a baby bath, put it on a firm surface. Waist-height is ideal to avoid having to bend and lift. If you put it on the floor, or in the big bath, hold your baby carefully before lifting him from the bath.

Bathing your newborn baby

It can be unnerving giving your baby her first bath, but with a little practise, you'll both enjoy the experience. For newborns, fill the bath with 5–8cm (2–3in) of water to cover your baby comfortably.

What you'll need

Have the following items ready before you start your baby's bath:

★ A baby bath set on a firm surface (your usual bath or a large basin will also do)

★ Two towels (one for wrapping while her hair is washed, and one for drying)

★ A thin flannel or sponge

★ Cotton wool

★ Baby wash and/or shampoo

★ A clean nappy

★ A clean set of clothes

TOP TIP

Young babies need a bath only two to three times a week. Avoid bathing her after a feed or when she is feeling tired or hungry, and keep bathtimes brief at first.

1 **Undress your baby and wrap her in a clean towel**. Cradle her on one arm with your hand supporting her head, lean her across the bath and wet her scalp or any hair with your hand or a wet flannel – lightly shampooed, if you wish. Rinse the flannel out and squeeze over her head to rinse.

2 **Remove the towel**, and with one hand supporting your baby's head and neck and the other supporting her bottom, slip her into the bath feet first. You can rest her head and neck on the palm of your hand or your forearm.

3 **Use a thin flannel** with a drop of baby bath if you wish to clean her neck and face and behind her ears. Clean her genitals and between her fingers and toes. Hold her towards you in the crook of your arm to wash her bottom and back.

4 **Lift her out of the bath** supporting her head and neck and holding her upper arm and bottom. Place her onto a towel and pat her dry immediately. Hold her close for a few minutes so that she feels warm and safe.

Reluctant bathers

Not all babies like bathtime, particularly in the early weeks. Choose a time when your baby is calm and alert. If she seems distressed by the prospect of a bath, simply top and tail her instead (see p.24) and try bathing another day. Here are some tips to ease your baby into bathtime.

Keep it sociable Sing and chat to your baby as you bathe her, and try to keep any anxiety you are feeling under wraps. Talk to her in a soothing voice, and explain what you are doing as you go.

A regular routine Make bathtime a part of your baby's routine as she grows to help her become accustomed to the process. If bathtime is always followed by a comforting feed, she will come to expect this to be a pleasurable time.

Fun and games A few brightly coloured bath toys can help to distract your baby if she becomes distressed.

A comfortable bath Make sure the bath water is nice and warm (but not too hot; it should be 35–38°C/95–100°F). A cold bath is certain to unsettle her.

Bathe together Try taking a bath with your baby. She'll be comforted by your presence and enjoy the skin-to-skin contact. If possible, ask someone else to lift her from the tub.

Help her feel secure Use a baby bath, basin or washing-up bowl if she finds a big bath daunting, to help her to feel safe. You could also try bathing her in a familiar room where she feeds or plays until she gets used to the idea that bathtime can be fun.

Checking the water The sensitive skin on your forearm is ideal for testing the temperature of your baby's bath. The water should feel comfortably warm.

Bathing your older baby

As your baby starts to become a little more mobile, and begins to eat solid food, he may need bathing more regularly. You could make a bath part of his bedtime routine so that he's clean, calm and ready for sleep.

Bathtime tips

Keep bathtime safe and fun with a few simple measures.

★ Once your baby is able to sit, a rubber safety mat and a bath seat are good investments, and your baby will enjoy being a little more independent.

★ Most babies love playing in the bath, so it's worth investing in a few sturdy bath toys to help him explore the wonderful world of water. Bath mitts that double up as puppets will keep him amused, and he'll enjoy tipping and refilling baby-sized buckets and watering cans. Sponges can provide endless fun and colourful shapes that stick onto the sides of the bath will fascinate him. You could keep them all in a net bag that hangs around the taps.

Baby seats These are available for sitting babies to help you wash your baby safely. However, no baby should be left alone in a seat, even for a few seconds.

Bathtime fun Playing in the bath encourages the development of your baby's motor skills, and increases his confidence in water. Choose toys that can be rinsed and dried.

KEY FACT
Your baby's bath is effectively his first swimming lesson, so help him to become confident in the water, and allow him to explore it, safe in your firm grip.

A firm hold Hold your baby's leg firmly when you lay him back: he may not be thrilled about being washed, and kick a little. Babies are very slippery when wet.

Getting out Some babies have so much fun in the tub, they don't want to get out. Make drying off fun; play rub-a-dub-dub with the towel, and give soothing massage strokes.

Washing your baby's hair

Your baby's hair needs to be washed about once a week. Try to avoid getting water in his eyes, since babies do tend to dislike this, and dry his hair straight after washing so he doesn't lose heat from his head.

Sponge washing Even bath-loving babies can resist having their hair washed. You may find it easier to use a sponge so that you can avoid water running down his face and he can remain upright.

Pouring jugs Jugs with a malleable lip protect your baby's face and eyes from water and shampoo, keeping them off his face. These are so effective you can often get on with the job without him noticing.

Detangling hair If your older baby has a plentiful head of hair, it's a good idea to brush it gently with a soft brush after washing it to help loosen any tangles. Use a baby brush with nice, soft bristles.

What can I do about cradle cap?

Many babies suffer from cradle cap when they are small. It's a type of dermatitis that usually appears in the first two months. It first appears as a red, scaly rash on the head, which over time can turn into thick, yellow scab-like scales.

Treating cradle cap Most cradle cap clears up on its own. However, you can ease any itching by massaging a little olive oil into your baby's scalp, leaving it overnight, then shampooing and, when dry, gently brushing away the loose scales with a soft brush. Try not to loosen crusts that have not pulled away on their own as this can cause bleeding and increase the risk of infection. In some cases, an antifungal or mild steroid cream may be necessary to control the condition and ease discomfort. Avoid frequent hair washing as this can worsen the condition.

Gentle treatment Rubbing olive oil into your baby's scalp helps to soften the flakes; don't be tempted to pull them off.

Cutting your baby's nails

It can be unnerving to cut your baby's tiny finger- and toenails, but keeping them short will help to stop him scratching himself (and you), and make it much easier to keep them clean.

Trimming tips

The following tips can help to remove the stress from nail cutting.

★ Find a comfortable position that allows you access to your baby's hands (or feet). You may find it easier to place him in his rocker or chair.

★ Always use nail scissors designed for babies, which have rounded ends that will not cut or prick him if he makes any sudden movement.

★ Hold your baby's palm and finger steady with one hand, while you cut his nails with the other.

★ It isn't necessary to file your baby's nails if you cut them short enough and keep the edges smooth.

★ If you accidentally cut him, don't panic. It's important to stay calm so that he doesn't associate nail-trimming with distress! Place a cotton ball or gauze pad over the site and press down for a few seconds. Never put a plaster on your baby's hands, as it can loosen when he puts his fingers in his mouth, and could cause choking.

Nail biting You may find it easier to nibble your baby's nails, perhaps when he is feeding and has a hand free. Take care not to peel the nails across, and use an emery board to smooth jagged edges.

Baby clippers Small-scale clippers designed for babies are ideal to trim nails quickly and efficiently. Do take care: it can be hard to manoeuvre your baby's tiny nails into the cutters, and you may end up nipping his skin instead.

Baby scissors Small round-tipped scissors are ideal for trimming your baby's nails. If your baby doesn't keep still when you cut his nails, you may find it easier to cut them when he is distracted by something else, or perhaps while he is asleep.

Team work It can be easier to trim your baby's nails if you both get involved. Hold your baby and try to distract him with soothing sounds while your partner trims his nails. He will probably enjoy the attention from both of you.

Looking after toenails

You'll need to keep an eye on your baby's toenails, too. Trimming them regularly helps to avoid problems.

Sensitive feet Your baby's feet may be ticklish, so rub them first before cutting his nails so that he is less sensitive to your touch.

Keep nails short It's important to keep your baby's toenails short to prevent them from snagging his skin and becoming ingrown. Ingrown toenails usually affect the big toe, which will look red and swollen around the nail. Cut toenails before they can break or tear.

Don't cut too much Don't cut his toenails too short, though. Always leave a little of the white showing at the end of the nail.

Using scissors Cut his toenails with round-tipped scissors or baby clippers. Cut straight across rather than rounding the edges, which can cause the nails to become ingrown.

Regular checking If your older baby starts to wear shoes, have the fit checked regularly. Your baby's feet will grow quickly, and shoes that are too small can damage not only his nails but also his toes.

Cleaning your baby's teeth

Your baby's first tooth can emerge any time from three months onwards, but typically emerges around six months. It's a good idea to introduce her to the idea of teeth brushing right from the beginning.

Good dental care

Gentle brushing with a first baby toothbrush should start as soon as her first tooth emerges.

★ Choose a toothbrush that is designed for your baby's age and size; a chubby handle makes it easier to grip.

★ Let your baby play with her toothbrush before brushing, so that it becomes familiar.

★ Brush in a circular motion, and brush her gums as well as her teeth.

★ Choose fluoride toothpaste for babies; dentists recommend that babies and young children should have at least 1000ppm of fluoride in their toothpaste.

★ Brush twice daily – once before bed, and at another time in the day. Try to leave at least half an hour after feeding, as your baby's saliva remineralizes her teeth, which makes them stronger.

★ Don't let your baby eat the toothpaste; too much fluoride can cause her teeth to become mottled.

★ Breastfeeding helps to keep teeth healthy. From six months, it's a good idea to introduce a cup. After one year, discourage drinking milk from a bottle, and give sweet foods only at mealtimes.

Using toothpaste Use a small smear of fluoride toothpaste on your baby's brush. Chances are that she will swallow it rather than spit it out, so it's important that she doesn't get too much (see box, left).

Good brushing Your baby may want to be involved, but you should brush her teeth at first, and continue to do so until she is competent at brushing, usually at about the age of seven. If it's easier, sit her on your lap and clean her teeth from behind.

Teething

Your baby may not show any signs of teething, or, indeed any teeth, until well into his first year of life. The process of teething often follows hereditary patterns, so if you or your partner teethed early or late, your baby may well do so too.

First signs Your baby may gnaw on his fingers when his teeth come through. Signs of teething can appear weeks before a tooth actually emerges, but you may be able to see a white bud on your baby's gums.

Teething rings Chewing on a chilled teething ring can soothe sore gums, or offer household items, such as a wooden spoon, to gnaw on. Choose rings that don't contain PVC or BPA, which can be toxic for babies.

A soothing rub Rub his gums with a clean finger, using a little teething gel to ease the discomfort. Many gels contain paracetamol, so take care that you don't use one at the same time as an oral dose for pain relief.

Cold treats Frozen fruit, such as melon or peaches, or hard vegetables, such as a carrot stick, can soothe any inflammation. You could also try freezing a wet flannel, which your baby can gnaw on or suck.

Signs of teething

Although some babies seem relatively untroubled by their teeth coming through, there are usually some clear indications that your baby's first tooth is on its way. You baby may show a combination of the following signs when he is teething.

★ Irritability and fussiness as his gums become sore and painful; the first tooth is often the worst

★ Drooling

★ Coughing or gagging as a result of extra saliva.

★ A rash on his chin, mainly due to the drooling.

★ Gnawing, gumming and biting everything he puts in his mouth.

★ Rubbing his cheeks and pulling his ears, as the pain travels to the ear area and around the jaw.

★ Mild diarrhoea. This is a contentious one, as some professionals think it's not linked, but a respected Australian study recently found that slightly looser bowel movements are a common symptom.

★ A slightly raised temperature. While a high fever is not a sign of teething, and should be treated as a caution, a low-grade fever can occur in some little ones. Again, some doctors disagree, but parents report that it's very common.

★ Poor sleep

★ A runny nose, as the ear, nose and throat area become a little inflamed.

Dressing your young baby

It's easy to get carried away when buying baby clothes, but your baby will soon outgrow them. Also, young babies spend most of their time in sleepsuits. Stick to basics, and save money for special occasion outfits.

Vests These are essential for babies. They keep babies warm in colder months, and can be worn on their own in summer with just a nappy. Choose cotton brands with poppers between the legs, and a wide neck.

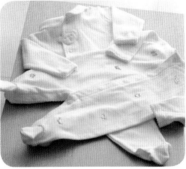

Sleepsuits These form the basis of your baby's wardrobe for at least the first few weeks. Choose loose-fitting, soft all-in-ones with poppers rather than buttons or zips, which can be fiddly or irritate your baby.

Hats These may be needed for premature babies until they have enough body fat to keep warm. Otherwise, save hats for outdoors only. Choose simple pull-on hats, or ones with a Velcro or popper fastening.

Socks These are useful to keep her toes warm when she's kicking in her vest. Buy cotton brands with firm ribbing – babies always kick off their socks! Soft shoes aren't necessary, but they can keep feet warm.

Layers You'll need one or two cardigans or jackets. Go for light ones that can be layered. Avoid layers that have to be pulled over the head. Poppers are easier than buttons and zips, which can irritate chins and necks.

Winter suit For cold weather, buy a light but warm all-in-one suit that zips or pops from the bottom of one leg to the neck. This allows you to remove the bottom half only for changes. Washable fabrics are essential!

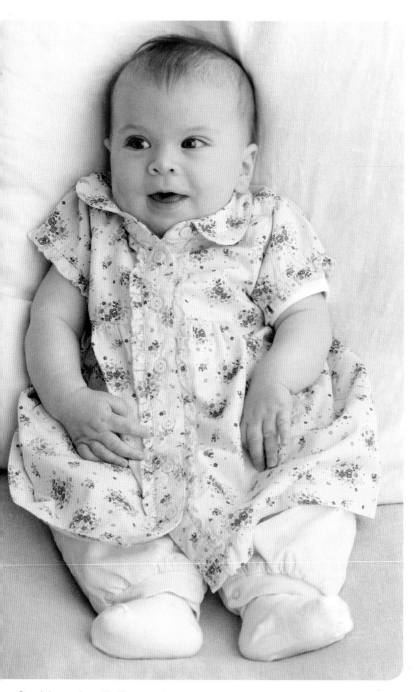

Your baby's laundry

Babies create lots of laundry! Here are a few tips to help you deal with stubborn stains and generally look after her clothes:

★ **Wash before wearing** Many clothes are finished with chemicals that can irritate a baby's skin, so do wash first; however, don't wash them all at once. You may find that your baby is bigger than you thought she might be, or grows more quickly. If you leave some of her wardrobe unwashed, and with original price tags, you can return them for a more appropriate size.

★ **Choose a non-biological washing powder or liquid** and put the clothing through an extra rinse cycle to be sure that no detergent remains. Some babies show no signs of irritation or discomfort when your usual detergent is used, but it's best to start off playing safe.

★ **If your baby has had a nappy leak** that has stained her clothes, soak them in an oxywash stain-removal solution overnight before washing. Avoid bleach, which could irritate your baby's skin.

★ **To remove stains** caused by breast milk, formula, blood, vomit and faeces, rub lemon juice into the stain, or soak in cold water with a cup of lemon juice.

★ **If the stain fails to loosen,** rub the area with washing-up liquid and leave overnight; then wash as normal.

★ **Let white clothing bleach** in the sun for a few hours, to lighten and brighten stubborn stains.

★ **Urine stains** can be treated by soaking in water with a tablespoon of ammonia to loosen, and then rub in a little washing-up liquid before washing.

★ **Avoid tumble-drying** anything that is still stained – the stain will set, and will become almost impossible to remove.

Special occasions You'll want at least one or two special outfits to show off your baby, but try to stick to practical, washable fabrics with easy access for nappy changes. Babies can be messy, no matter what the occasion.

Putting on your baby's vest

A vest is a wardrobe staple for both the winter and summer months. It's easiest to dress your baby when he is lying on his back, but you can undertake quick changes when he's well supported on your lap.

Top tips

Young babies often object to being undressed and dressed. Following these tips can help to make dressing him an efficient and stress-free process.

★ You may wish to lay a towel on the change mat if it's cold. If you don't have a change mat, a towel will suffice.

★ In the early weeks, dress your baby in easy-to-open clothing, which can be removed with the minimum of fuss.

★ Remember that many babies dislike being changed, so coo, smile and sing to him in a reassuring voice throughout to help ease his fears.

★ You may wish to hang a mobile or toy over the changing area to distract him.

★ Keep a basket for dirty laundry next to your changing station to make laundry time that much easier.

TOP TIP

For young babies, simple styles of vests and suits are best. Frills, ribbons or ties can easily get caught around little fingers and necks.

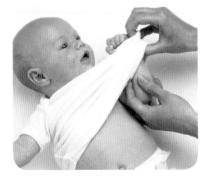

1 **Stretch the neck** opening of the vest so that it's wide enough to go over his head. Talk to him or sing so that he isn't alarmed by the process, and make soothing noises if he is distressed.

2 **Gently pull the vest** over his head, lifting and supporting his head from the back. Pull one arm of the vest outwards, and ease his hand into the sleeve. Cup his hand to keep his fingers together.

3 **Repeat with the other arm,** and then smooth the vest down over his body to smooth out uncomfortable wrinkles. Check the neck area to ensure that it's flush against his skin.

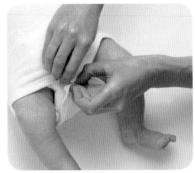

4 **Do up the poppers** at the base of your baby's vest, and then run your fingers around the inside leg to be sure that there is space for him to move his legs comfortably.

Putting on your baby's sleepsuit

Your baby may need several changes each day, and during the night. It may seem like an impossible feat to squeeze her tiny body into a fiddly sleepsuit, but work from the bottom up and she'll be dressed in no time.

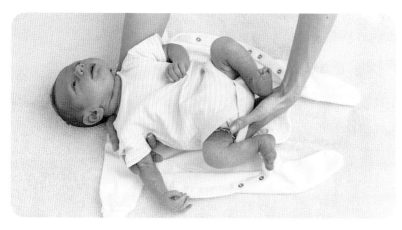

1 **Lay your baby's sleepsuit** down on a flat surface with the poppers open and facing upwards. Gently place your baby on the sleepsuit, reassuring her as you do so.

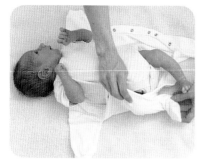

2 **Guide a foot** into the sleepsuit leg. Pull it up her leg so that her toes are at the end of the suit. Repeat with her other foot. Smooth the suit over her legs. Do up the poppers to just below the waist.

3 **Pull one sleeve out** and slide her hand into the sleeve; pull it out with your other hand. Repeat with the other arm. Smooth the fabric so that the poppers meet, and carefully do them up.

How much clothing?

You may think that your baby needs layers of clothing and blankets to keep warm, but this isn't the case.

Hot or cold You can tell if your baby is too warm by placing your hand on her tummy – if this feels hot to the touch, remove a layer of clothes. Don't worry if her hands and feet feel cool as this is normal.

What your baby wears Most young babies need hats – a warm one for outdoors in the winter, and a hat with a brim to keep the sun off the skin on her face. A vest, a sleepsuit and a cardigan are ideal for cool days. If the temperature rises, remove a layer of clothes. In the summer, she will probably be happy wearing a vest, or a simple sleepsuit with no vest.

When she sleeps A vest, sleepsuit and light cotton blanket are usually sufficient for sleeping in the colder months. You can fold the blanket for extra warmth on very cold nights. In the warmer months, remove layers as required.

Dressing your older baby

As your baby grows, his needs will change. He may be ready for proper clothes, rather than all-in-ones. Aim for practicality. It won't be long before your baby is mobile, and he'll need comfortable, sturdy clothing.

Sensible hats Choose a hat with a Velcro strap under the chin. Strings are fiddly and potentially dangerous. In winter, find jackets and tops with hoods, or keep your baby's head warm with a woollen hat.

First shoes Babies do not need shoes until they're walking confidently, but you can keep her feet warm with bootees or soft leather moccasin-type footwear. Shoes with elasticized tops help keep her socks on, too.

Easy openings Most babies dislike having clothes pulled over their heads, so make the job easier by choosing tops and jumpers with poppers at the neck. This also makes it easier to remove clothing if he falls asleep!

Clothes for crawling Choose loose, comfortable clothing that allows your baby to explore her surroundings without being restricted. Look for padding in the knee area, and plenty of room in the legs and arms.

Keeping her still While it may be easier to dress your baby when she is on her back, her new mobility means that she may not stay there. Dress her on your lap, talking to her and making a game of the proceedings.

Adding layers Dressing your baby in thin layers is preferable to bulky, heavy clothing that restricts his movement. Layers are ideal when you're out, allowing you to add or take off clothing as needed.

Top dressing tips

Follow these tips to make dressing as stress-free as possible for you both.

★ He'll still need regular changing, so make sure that pants and other items are easy to remove and put on.

★ Avoid anything too fussy that will irritate the skin or get in the way of your baby's activities.

★ Poppers and well-padded zips are easier than buttons.

★ Make sure that any tops and jumpers have wide necks.

★ Make your life easier by choosing machine-washable clothes.

★ Vests with poppers under the crotch will keep your baby warm when T-shirts or dresses ride up.

★ If she constantly loses her socks, why not consider a pair of tights. This also works for boys!

★ Try to buy most of your socks in the same colour, so you don't face an endless pile of odd socks. And there's nothing wrong with mismatched socks from time to time – just call it your baby's unique sense of style.

TOP TIP
Once your baby is mobile, consider choosing a wardrobe in complementary colours, so that leaks and spills don't mean a whole new outfit!

The art of distraction If your baby is annoyed by having to stop her explorations to get dressed, make it fun for her. Talk about her socks, wiggle her toes and play "This little piggy". If all else fails, distract her with a toy while you dress her.

Putting safety first

It goes without saying that keeping your baby safe and well is your first priority, and you'll want to take every precaution. It's easier to enjoy life with your baby if you're confident that you've covered all the bases.

Being alert

Looking after your baby means being constantly vigilant. Keep in mind the guidelines below for peace of mind that you're doing your best to keep her safe.

★ Supervise your baby at all times – don't get distracted. Never leave her unattended on a bed or raised surface.

★ Be aware that accidents are more likely to happen when you're tired, under stress, or during periods of change, such as when you're on holiday. Be extra vigilant at such times.

★ Keep your baby out of the kitchen as much as you can, or have a "safe" play space for her.

★ As well as keeping hot drinks away from your baby, get into the habit now of turning the handles of your saucepans inwards, so that she can't reach up and pull them down.

★ Keep anything that could be a choking hazard for your baby, such as small toys, beads or marbles, well away from areas where your baby plays, sleeps or feeds.

Your baby's pushchair This should have a five-point harness, and it's really important to do it all up every time you go out – even for short trips. She can topple out if you overload your buggy, or turn a steep corner.

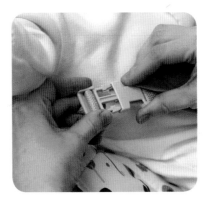

Safety straps Always use the safety straps on seats. Even if your baby isn't mobile, it's important to keep her securely strapped in as she may wriggle. Strap your older baby into her highchair to stop her climbing out.

Avoiding scalds It's crucial to keep hot drinks away from your baby. Push them back from the table edge or away from your baby if she is sitting at the table. Never hold your baby and a hot drink at the same time.

Extra care When your baby first learns to sit up, put cushions around her in case she topples over. Watch, though, that she doesn't become trapped face down on a cushion.

Babyproofing your home

Babies have a habit of developing new skills quickly, and before you know it, he may be rolling or pulling himself up. Make sure that he is protected from potential accidents, which can happen in any home. There are lots of easy ways to make your home a safe environment for your baby to explore.

Safety tips

Keep your home environment safe by following the guidelines below.

★ Switch off all electrics at night and close doors. Plan your actions in the case of a fire; keep matches and lighters out of the reach of children, and stub out any cigarettes.

★ Keep all lamps and everything else electrical at least one metre from your baby's bed.

★ Tie up electric flexes so they cannot be pulled. Make sure all cords for appliances and electrical equipment, as well as blinds and curtains, are tied up or well out of reach.

★ Get a fire guard if your fireplace or heater is in regular use.

★ Ensure that safety gates conform to British safety standard BS 4125. Install gates at the top and bottom of stairways and kitchen door as needed.

★ Secure bookshelves and chests of drawers to the wall – many babies become avid climbers very early on!

★ Ensure that there are no strings or cords hanging near your baby's bed, changing table, play area or chair.

★ Remove mobiles from your baby's cot when he can reach up and touch them.

★ Avoid using pillows, thick bedding, or anything electric in your baby's cot.

★ Keep your floors clear of objects and tack down rugs; it's easy to trip when you are tired and carrying your baby.

Socket covers It's important to cover the plug sockets throughout the house with plastic covers. Babies will often explore the moment your back is turned. Before you know it, your baby will be rolling, crawling or shuffling, so play safe and be ready.

Safely locked away Fit childproof locks on all cupboards that your baby can reach once he's mobile. Most importantly, it's crucial to keep him away from potentially poisonous products, such as cleaning supplies, alcohol and toiletries.

Out of reach Place any medications, chemical cleaning supplies, alcohol, laundry supplies, matches and toiletries in a child-locked cupboard – and preferably one that cannot be reached by your mobile baby.

Smoke alarms Fit smoke alarms at every level of your home. Look for one with a combined carbon monoxide alarm, which alerts you when levels of this dangerous gas are too high. Check the batteries regularly.

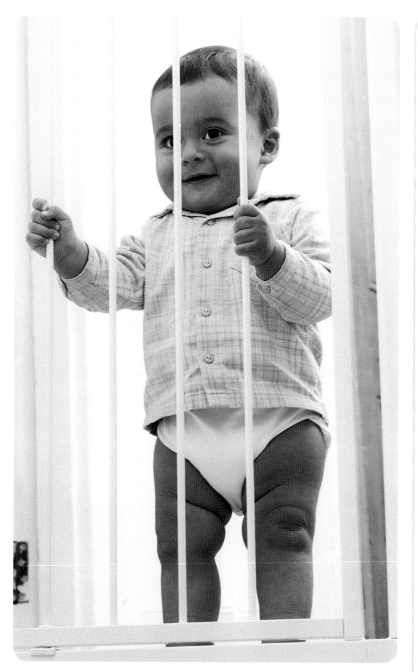

Safety in the garden

Once your baby is mobile, you'll need to check that your outside space is a safe environment, too.

Constant supervision It is very important to watch your baby at all times. Babies can manoeuvre themselves into awkward positions, or make a quick escape if the garden gate is left open.

Garden hazards Make sure that pot plants, lawn fertilizers and other gardening chemicals are out of reach, as well as anything that could contain water, such as a watering can. Ponds and swimming pools should have fences and gates around them and, ideally, be covered.

Off he goes Once your baby starts to explore beyond his immediate environment, you'll need to evaluate safety in your garden or patio areas.

Avoiding falls A stairgate keeps your baby from falling down the stairs. Ensure it's firmly fitted and won't come loose if your child plays with it. When carrying your baby up and down stairs, hold him securely in one arm and hold the handrail firmly with your free hand.

When your baby is unwell

Babies' immune systems are still developing, making them susceptible to illness. They normally recover quickly but knowing what to look for will help you feel more confident about what (if any) action you should take.

First sign It's usually obvious when your baby is unwell. The first sign is often a fever (see p.50). She'll need lots of comfort; babies can become very distressed, and may want to be held constantly.

Feeling hot It's better to feel the back of your baby's neck rather than her forehead when assessing whether she feels hot.

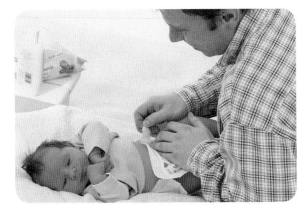

Losing fluids Babies can dehydrate quickly, particularly if they've had vomiting or diarrhoea. Check her nappies. She should have at least six very wet ones each day, and at least one bowel movement.

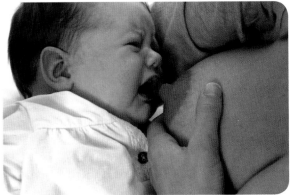

Feeling unsettled If your baby is reluctant to feed for several hours, see your doctor. Breastfeeding helps her fight off infection. It will also keep her hydrated and topped up with nutrients.

Taking your baby's temperature

You may know instinctively when your baby has a fever: he might be irritable or drowsy, look flushed and his tummy, back and neck may feel hot. You may wish to take his temperature for confirmation.

Under-arm digital thermometer A digital thermometer is used under your baby's arm. Hold it in place for the specified time to give an accurate reading. They can be difficult to use on a wriggling baby.

Digital ear thermometer These give an almost instantaneous reading, but they are expensive. Make sure you read the instructions carefully, as it's important to place the thermometer correctly in the ear.

Assessing your baby

Not all babies have a fever when they are ill, so it's worth looking out for other signs that could indicate that he isn't well. Contact your doctor if your baby has any of the following symptoms:

★ Weak or very excessive crying

★ Lack of interest in his usual feeds

★ Failure to smile as usual

★ Sleeps for unusually long periods

★ Irritability

★ Fewer wet nappies than usual

★ An unusual rash

★ Vomiting and diarrhoea; the most common causes of dehydration, which is dangerous in babies. Watch out for sunken eyes, pallor, fewer wet nappies, and a depressed fontanelle.

Obtaining an accurate reading

Depending on the type of thermometer, you can take your baby's temperature under the armpit, in the ear, or on the forehead. But which method gives the most accurate results?

Ear thermometers These are accurate provided they are placed correctly in the ear. If your baby has been out in the cold, or lying on a pillow, wait 10–15 minutes before taking a reading.

Probe thermometers: armpit method Armpit readings are not the most reliable. However, since probe thermometers can't be used orally on babies or small children (there's a risk they might bite them) the armpit method is more suitable and safe.

Forehead strips These measure the skin – rather than body – temperature, so are not particularly accurate. However, they are convenient, especially if your baby won't sit still. Hold the strip on your baby's forehead for a couple of minutes.

KEY FACT

Temperature control isn't well developed in babies, and their temperature can rise and fall quickly. Trust your instincts and call the doctor if you think your baby is unwell.

Dealing with a fever

In most cases, babies develop a fever as they're fighting infection; other reasons for a high temperature include being overdressed, teething and immunizations. In babies, a temperature above 38°C (100.4°F) is high.

When to call your doctor

Contact the doctor if your baby's symptoms are causing you any concern. Always call if your baby has:

★ A fever that is higher than 38°C (100.4°F) if she is under three months old; or 39°C (102.2°F) if she is between three and six months old

★ Other signs of illness as well as a raised temperature

Seek immediate medical help if your baby has any of the following:

★ A stiff neck

★ Abnormally rapid breathing

★ Abnormal drowsiness

★ Unusual irritability

★ Refuses to drink

★ Persistent vomiting or diarrhoea

★ Has a convulsion (seizure)

★ She cannot be comforted

★ A dark red or purple rash, which does not fade when a glass is pressed against her skin.

Topping up fluids If your baby has a fever, she will need extra fluids to replace those lost through illness. Offer as much water as you can. Don't worry if she eats less when unwell: it's more important to stay hydrated.

Keep feeding Breastfed babies with a fever should be fed more often than usual to avoid dehydration. If dehydration continues, both breast- and bottle-fed babies may need a rehydration solution to replace lost fluids.

The right measure When giving your baby medicine, always follow the instructions on the packet, as too much can make her ill. Talk to your doctor or the pharmacist if you're unsure what dose to give.

Restorative sleep Your baby may sleep more than usual when she's ill, which is part of the healing process. Make sure that she is kept cool and check her regularly to see how she is doing.

A comforting hug Babies need plenty of
reassurance when they're ill; taking time to comfort
her will help to relax and soothe her.

Giving medicine

It's sometimes necessary to give your baby medicine to reduce a fever or deal with infection. Most babies don't take kindly to medicine, but you will soon become adept at giving it efficiently. Follow the instructions, and if antibiotics are prescribed, make sure he finishes the course.

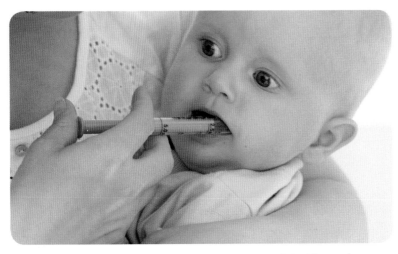

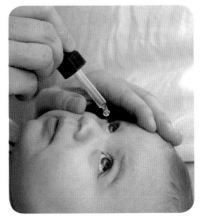

Eye drops Wash your hands. Get your baby into position with his head tilted back. Gently pull down his lower lid; hold the dropper above his eye (take care not to touch his eye) and squeeze one drop into his lower eyelid.

Using a syringe This is the easiest way to give medicine to your baby. Measure the dose, put the syringe in his mouth and slowly squirt the contents into his cheek – not the back of his mouth, as this may cause choking.

Over-the-counter medications

Your doctor or pharmacist will let you know which medications and doses are suitable for your baby, based on his age and overall health. Don't assume that natural or complementary medicines are safe for your baby – you should always check with your doctor before using them.

What's right for your baby Some medicines aren't appropriate for babies under two or three months old without a doctor's permission, including ibuprofen and paracetamol, which reduce fever and offer pain relief. Ibuprofen acts as an anti-inflammatory, which can help inflammatory conditions such as ear infections and sore throats. Paracetamol works to reduce a high fever.

Rehydration solutions These may be useful in the event of diarrhoea or vomiting, although they are usually only required for babies who are bottle-fed. Always make up the solution according to the manufacturer's instructions.

Cough medicine and decongestants These medicines are not advised for babies or young children under six years old.

Antifungal treatments These are used to treat thrush, which is common in babies' mouths. If you breastfeed, your nipple will also need treating.

Steroid creams Mild steroid creams, such as hydrocortisone, may be advised for very itchy, inflamed skin, or severe nappy rash. Use sparingly, and only when absolutely necessary.

Your baby's immunizations

Your baby will have a series of routine immunizations, or vaccinations, over his first year to help prevent childhood illnesses. After a vaccination, keep your baby cool, offer extra fluids and give your baby paracetamol if he has a mild fever. If your baby experiences any other symptoms, call your doctor for advice.

★ 2 months	Diphtheria, tetanus, whooping cough, polio, and haemophilus influenza type b immunizations in one injection (DTaP/IPV/Hib); injection to protect against pneumococcal infection (PCV)
★ 3 months	DTaP/IPV/Hib (second dose); immunization against meningitis C in a separate injection (MenC)
★ 4 months	DTaP/IPV/Hib (third dose); another MenC; another PCV
★ Around 12 months	Another DTaP/IPV/Hib plus MenC, in one injection
★ Around 13 months	Vaccination for measles, mumps and rubella in one injection (MMR); another PCV

A dosage spoon This can be used to give medicine, but it's easy to spill the contents if your baby resists. Try offering it just before a regular feed. Tip little amounts into his mouth so that it goes in drop by drop. Stroke and reassure him.

Giving medicines safely

Follow the guidelines below when giving your baby medication.

★ **Shake the bottle** before measuring the dose.

★ **Note any side effects** that your baby experiences, and let your doctor know.

★ **Never give your baby** medication designed for older children, or anything prescribed for another child.

★ **Don't give aspirin** to babies (or any child under 16), as it can cause a serious illness known as Reye's syndrome.

★ **If you give your baby too much medicine** in error, tell your doctor or pharmacist, who will advise you of the best course of action.

★ **Never give more than is recommended** on the label. If dosage is worked out by your baby's weight, ask someone to double-check your calculations to be sure you're right.

★ **Keep an eye on the clock,** and don't administer medicine more often than prescribed. If you are using an over-the-counter medicine, it's important not to use it more often than suggested.

Feeding your baby

YOUR BABY'S NEEDS

Milk forms the basis of your baby's diet for the first year of her life, even once she has started on solid foods. Breast milk is by far the best food for your baby, with a host of benefits; but if you're unable to breastfeed, bottlefeeding provides all the nutrients your baby needs.

BREAST IS BEST A great deal of research has been undertaken into the benefits of breastfeeding, and it's clear that it provides the perfect start for your baby, affecting her health and development on many levels.

The composition of breast milk changes constantly, adapting to your baby's needs. Research shows that breastfed babies have fewer incidences of vomiting and diarrhoea, and that they're protected against gastroenteritis, as well as ear infections, respiratory illnesses, pneumonia, bronchitis, kidney infections and septicaemia (blood poisoning). There is also a reduced risk of constipation and other tummy disorders.

The fat contained in human milk, compared with cow's milk, is more digestible for babies, allowing greater absorption of fat-soluble vitamins into the bloodstream from the intestine. This is important because healthy fats, including essential fatty acids, are necessary for healthy growth and optimum development, particularly in the brain. Breast milk also promotes growth because of the presence of certain hormones.

There is a reduced risk of childhood diabetes in breastfed babies, as well as protection against allergies, asthma and eczema. Most important, though, there is a reduced risk of SIDS (Sudden Infant Death Syndrome); research showed that of every 87 deaths from SIDS, only three took place in breastfed babies. The emotional benefits are great too, as breastfed babies enjoy a very close connection with their mothers, and skin-to-skin contact nurtures bonding.

SUCCESSFUL BREASTFEEDING Some women adjust to breastfeeding very quickly and easily; others find that it takes a little longer, but once underway, it's enjoyable, convenient and usually problem-free. You can also relax in the knowledge that your baby will grow and develop at optimum levels. In this chapter, there's guidance on ensuring that your baby gets what she needs, when she needs it, as well as solutions for common concerns.

Studies show that women who feed on demand are likely to breastfeed for longer. Feeding on demand also prevents problems with milk supply, and encourages emotional security, as you're meeting your baby's needs as and when she needs you to.

It's important to look after yourself when you are breastfeeding. A balanced

The best start Breastfeeding your baby gives her the best possible nutritional start in life as well as having benefits for you too.

A comfortable feed Taking a break to burp your baby mid-feed helps to keep her comfortable and may reduce possetting.

Bottle-feeding Whether your baby is breastfed or on formula milk, bottles give dads the chance to take a turn at feeding.

and nutritious diet ensures that your baby gets the nutrients she needs from your milk, and that you stay healthy, relaxed and full of energy. Include plenty of wholegrains, fresh fruit and vegetables, lean meat, fish and poultry, and healthy snacks. Keeping blood-sugar levels stable with regular, healthy meals will not only keep up your milk supply, but also your energy and mood!

BOTTLE-FEEDING For mothers who are unable to breastfeed, formula milk provides babies with all of the nutrients they need. It's essentially a mix of water, carbohydrate, protein, fat, vitamins and minerals, and meets your baby's needs for both fluid and food. Bottlefeeding enables you to measure how much milk your baby is taking in and, because formula is digested more slowly than breast milk, bottle-fed infants may sleep longer. We'll look at all you need to know about bottlefeeding (pp.74–75).

STARTING SOLIDS Before you know it, your baby will be ready for her first solid food, around the six-month mark. At first, introducing solids is about getting used to new tastes and textures – it's an exciting time for you both. We'll guide you through the weaning process to ensure that your baby gets the nutrients she needs to thrive.

Moving onto solids Weaning your baby onto solid foods is a thrilling time for both her and you. Her world is opening up as she experiences new tastes and textures, and sociable family mealtimes can really begin now.

Taking control By 12 months, your baby will be drinking happily from her own cup as her independence grows.

Your growing baby

In the first months, your baby grows at an amazing rate and his appearance changes on an almost daily basis. On average, babies double their birth weight by three to four months and triple it by their first birthday.

Formula feeds Bottle-feeding is an option for mums who don't wish to breastfeed (or can't), and it offers some freedom from feeding. Make it a nurturing experience: hold your baby close so he feels secure.

Thriving baby It's natural to be concerned that your baby is growing at the right rate. Rest assured that if he's gaining weight, is alert, has regular wet and dirty nappies and a good skin tone, he's doing well.

A perfect balance Breast milk supplies your baby with just the right amount of nutrients, as well as antibodies, fatty acids, water and amino acids for his digestion, brain development and growth. For many women, established nursing also feels wonderful because it brings you and your baby close.

UK WHO growth charts for breastfed babies

New growth charts were recently produced for the UK, in an attempt to promote breastfeeding and discourage childhood obesity. The charts provide more accurate measurements for the growth of breastfed babies, as these babies put on weight at a slower rate than those who are bottlefed.

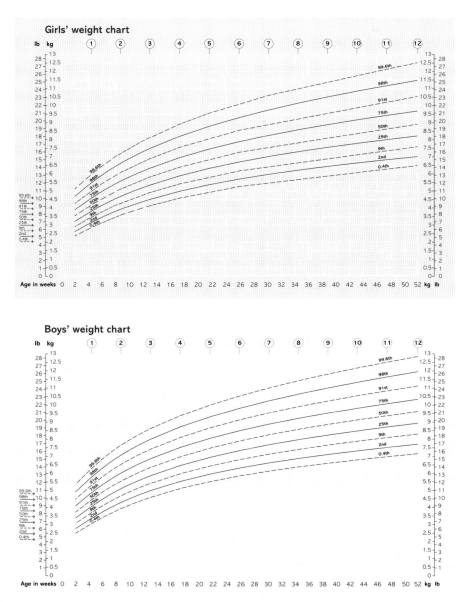

Girls' weight chart

Boys' weight chart

A permanent record You'll be given a growth chart, usually with your baby's record book, upon which you can plot her weight. The chart is broken up into "centiles". These charts work on averages so being on the "50th centile" for weight means your baby is absolutely average for her age; being under the "50th centile" indicates that she is lighter than average for her age.

Growing well Plotting these figures ensures that your baby remains on much the same line as she grows. However, if she is alert, gaining weight, sleeping well, and is content, she is growing properly.

Key to charts
— Centiles
○ Age in months

Data sources
UK 1990 reference data, reanalysed 2009 and WHO Child Growth Standards (WHO Multicentre Growth Reference Study Group).

Starting to breastfeed

Although breastfeeding is a natural process, there are a few "aids" to help ensure that feeding your baby runs as smoothly as possible for you both.

TOP TIP

Always bring your baby to the breast (see p.62), rather than the other way around. Have a glass of water or juice by your side to keep you hydrated during a feed.

A good support You'll need at least two nursing bras, professionally fitted, if possible. Look for supportive bras with fastenings that can be opened with one hand.

Breast pumps There is a wide variety of pumps; you may need to experiment to find which one you prefer. Electric pumps are efficient, but some find them invasive.

Nipple shields These can be useful in the short term if you have sore, cracked or inverted nipples but they can make it harder for babies to get milk.

Gel pads Absorbent gel pads soothe the nipple area if you have discomfort. Keep them in the freezer or fridge and then pop them inside your bra after a feed.

Breast pads and creams Pads are helpful if your breasts leak. Choose ones without a plastic backing, which can irritate. Lanolin-based creams can help soothe sore nipples.

Feeding cushion A V-shaped cushion is ideal for breastfeeding as it supports your back, baby and arms. As some feeds can last a while, comfort is a must!

Skin-to-skin contact Close contact straight after the birth helps to promote bonding and to establish breastfeeding, as well as stabilizing your baby's temperature, breathing, heart rate and blood sugar.

Night-time feeds Despite what other mums might say, all young babies need to feed at night and will continue to do so for the first few months. Keeping the lights dim and changing her nappy before a feed may help her get back to sleep afterwards.

Dispelling breastfeeding myths

The sheer volume of breastfeeding advice you receive can be confusing, so it's important to be able to distinguish fact from fiction. Here are some of the most common misconceptions…

Myth: Many women don't produce enough milk. In fact, very few women don't produce enough, and the majority produce more than is needed. The most common reason for babies not getting the milk is poor latching on (see p.62).

Myth: It's normal for feeding to be painful. A little tenderness is common for the first few days as your nipples become accustomed to the suckling. However, this should be temporary and it should never be painful enough to cause distress or inhibit feeding. If you do experience pain, it is almost always caused by poor latching on.

Myth: Babies may need formula to supplement colostrum. Before breast milk comes in, colostrum or "first milk" provides all the nutritional goodness your baby needs, as well as beneficial antibodies and bacteria. Nothing else is needed.

Myth: Breastfed babies may need extra water, especially when it's hot. Breast milk contains all the liquid your baby needs in any weather.

Myth: Breast milk doesn't contain enough iron. Full-term babies get enough iron from breast milk to last for at least six months. What's more, the iron in breast milk is "bioavailable", which means that your baby assimilates it more easily than the iron contained in formula milk.

Myth: It's easier to bottle-feed than breastfeed. Breastfeeding is often perceived to be hard at the outset. Once established, though, it couldn't be easier, with milk available when needed.

Myth: Breastfed babies don't sleep as well as bottle-fed babies. While it's true that breastfed babies may wake more often for feeds at first, once they are able to latch on well for a full feed before bed, they sleep just as well as bottle-fed babies.

Latching on

Making sure that your baby's mouth is in the right position and properly attached to your breast is key to successful breastfeeding. There's a bit of technique to getting it right but once he's latched on correctly you'll feel comfortable and assured that he's getting all the milk he needs.

1 **Sit in a supportive chair**, with your back straight and lap flat. Hold your baby facing you, and support his back and head with your hand: your thumb by one ear, your forefinger by the other ear, and your other fingers under his armpit.

2 **Take the weight** of your baby in your forearm and, with your other hand, tuck his legs under the elbow opposite to the side that he will feed on. He is now positioned with his tummy facing yours – the "tummy to mummy" position.

3 **Position your baby's nose** opposite your nipple. Make sure that your baby's arm is around your body, rather than tucked under your breast, then allow his head to tilt back slightly and wait for his mouth to open wide.

Signs that your baby is feeding well

★ He has a good colour, is gaining weight and is alert and looks around.

★ He has at least six wet nappies a day.

★ Breastfed babies' bowel motions are soft and runny after the fourth day and can occur twice daily. Occasionally they're less frequent, but if all else is well, this is unlikely to be a problem.

★ You hear a soft swallowing noise, rather than "sucking" when he feeds.

★ He is content and satisfied after most feeds, coming off the breast by himself.

★ Your breasts and nipples aren't sore.

4 **Once your baby's mouth is wide open**, with his tongue down and forwards and your nipple aimed at the roof of his mouth, quickly lift him up and on to your breast.

5 **Your baby now has a big mouthful of breast**. His lower lip is rolled out, his chin touching your breast, and he's breathing easily. Cradle him in your arms as he makes slow, deep sucks.

A relaxing feed When you're establishing breastfeeding, you will need to offer your baby both breasts at each feed, so that you stimulate your breasts to produce sufficient milk to meet your baby's needs. Try to relax while you're breastfeeding. Think about your milk flow and simply gaze at your baby, as this will help to stimulate the let-down reflex and release your milk.

Getting comfortable

Although breastfeeding is one of the most natural acts, it can take practice! Both you and your baby need to get used to different positions. As long as her tummy is against you, and she's latched on well, it's fine to experiment.

Before you start

Although breastfeeding doesn't require any equipment as such, it's a good idea to get a few things ready before you settle down to feed:

★ **A comfortable chair** with a footstool, or something else to raise your feet.

★ **Pillows** to ensure that you are comfortable as you support your baby.

★ **A glass of water** or another refreshing drink: breastfeeding is thirsty work!

★ **A small snack.** In the beginning your baby will need frequent feeds, and it can help to keep your energy levels up by nibbling on something healthy.

★ **A muslin** to clear up any possetting or leaking milk.

★ **Breast pads** may be useful if you find you're leaking milk.

The cradle hold Once you've lifted your baby up and on to the breast, you can cradle her with her tummy against yours and her head in the crook of your elbow. Keep her ear, shoulders and hip in a straight line. Tuck her lower arm around you.

KEY FACT
Your milk usually comes in two to six days after the birth. If it's slower, try not to worry. Put your baby to the breast frequently. Your midwife or health visitor will monitor her growth.

Side by side Latch your baby onto the breast, then position both you and your baby on your sides, with your tummies together to continue the feed. For comfort and support, bend your top leg and put pillows under your upper knee.

The rugby hold Position your baby with her legs and body under your arm, your hand under her head and neck. Let her latch on while pulling her close, holding her head, with her nose and chin touching your breast.

Feeding after a Caesarean

Some women find it hard to feed after a Caesarean, either because of the discomfort, or because of the medication.

Getting comfortable It might take a bit longer for your milk to come in, as the vaginal birth process gets things going, but your baby will get all she needs from your colostrum. You may need to feed her every two hours to stimulate milk production. Using a V-shaped pillow to support her, or lying on your side can be easier than having her weight on your abdomen. Ask for pain relief that is safe to use during breastfeeding.

Feeding twins

Although some mothers feel concerned about feeding two babies, it's certainly possible to breastfeed twins – and exclusively, if you wish to do so. Rest assured that your body will make ample milk for both of your babies, even if this seems like an impossibility at the outset.

Feeding two babies is challenging, but there are a number of ways that it can be undertaken successfully. Don't hesitate to get help from your midwife, health visitor or breastfeeding counsellor on your positioning. Babies are individuals and rarely follow the same schedule. Feeding twins takes time to master, and it's often easier to feed them individually at first. Once you're confident and their sleeping and feeding patterns start to merge, you can try feeding them together. When you settle down to feed, relax, focus on your babies and tune out the rest of the world.

When feeding twins, your calorie needs are greater. Eat complex carbohydrates, such as healthy breakfast cereals, to sustain energy, and drink plenty of fluids.

Double feed The rugby hold is popular for twins. Invest in a V-shaped pillow that supports your twins without putting pressure on your abdomen.

Feeding on demand

Feeding on demand helps to establish your milk supply. From time to time your baby will be hungrier and require longer and more frequent feeds. This is a good sign that he is thriving on your milk.

Feeding during growth spurts

Your baby will grow and develop at a rapid pace in his first year, and may seem hungrier than usual at times.

Supply and demand Many breastfeeding mums are tempted to give up breastfeeding during growth spurts because they feel anxious that they're not producing enough milk. However, this is very rarely the case.

Phases of rapid growth occur every few weeks, with major growth spurts normally occurring around three weeks, six weeks, three months and six months. You'll need to feed him more frequently during these times to build up your milk supply to meet his demands. This normally only takes 24 to 48 hours, so don't panic.

KEY FACT
Emptying one breast before moving on to the next means that your baby gets both the thirst-quenching foremilk, and the more calorific and nutritious hind milk.

Reading the signs Over time, you'll learn to understand your baby's cues for hunger or thirst. He needs feeding about eight to 12 times a day for the first month or so, so chances are he's hungry when he cries.

Ready for bed Encourage your baby to feed from both breasts in the evening: if he has a full tummy, he may sleep for longer. However, newborns should not go longer than four hours between feeds.

Keep up your strength Eat three healthy, well-balanced meals each day while feeding, with plenty of good-quality snacks, such as fruit, nuts, wholegrain sandwiches, soup and vegetables in between.

Power naps Frequent night wakings take their toll and tiredness makes breastfeeding harder work, so make every attempt to rest or nap when your baby sleeps, no matter how many other things need your attention.

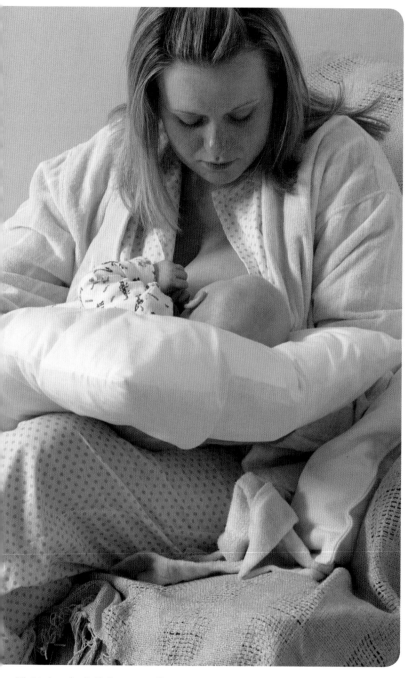

Night-time feeds Before your milk supply is fully established, it's important to feed your baby on demand, even in the night. In many cases, babies will go a little longer at night, particularly if they have a good long feed prior to bedtime.

Comfort feeding

Many babies love the comfort of breastfeeding, and when all else fails it can often be the best way to soothe your baby.

Starting out At the outset, it can be difficult to tell the difference between a hungry baby and one who is feeding for comfort, but you'll soon realise when he is snacking rather than having a full feed. Generally, a feed takes 20–40 minutes, and newborns need around 10–12 feeds in a 24-hour period. By one month, if your baby is gaining weight well, he will be feeding every two to three hours. If your baby is getting only a little drink before he falls asleep, he's likely to wake soon, demanding more – a process that can go on all day and night! It's best to gently nudge him, and switch positions, to encourage him to keep suckling. Try to feed your baby when he's hungry and alert, when he'll take more.

Other forms of comfort It's a good idea to get into the habit of cuddling your baby, and singing to or playing with him when he's unhappy. This way, your baby will learn that there are other ways to feel good that don't involve milk!

Breastfeeding problems

Every mother and baby's experience is different, and some mums find it hard to get their baby latched on well, which can be painful. If you have any problems, talk to your midwife or a breastfeeding counsellor.

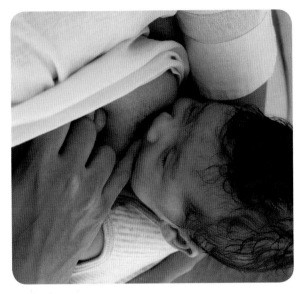

1 **If you have discomfort** over and above a little tenderness, your baby may not be latched on well (see pp.62–63). Insert a clean finger in the corner of her mouth to break the suction.

2 **Reposition her carefully,** with her mouth wide open and the whole of your nipple and some of the breast tissue in her mouth. Take her to your breast, not your breast to her.

Preventing and treating mastitis

Mastitis is an inflammation of the breast tissue, usually caused by severe engorgement. The condition normally affects one breast only, causing it to become red, painful and swollen. You may notice hot or red streaks on your breast, and you may have a raised temperature.

Emptying the breast As mastitis usually occurs because of engorgement, it's important to ensure that your baby is correctly latched on and able to drain your breast completely. If it isn't obvious, try to keep a note of the breast on which your baby fed last, so that each breast is fully emptied, even if not in one sitting.

Symptoms These may be so uncomfortable that you're tempted to stop breastfeeding; however, it is important that you continue. Regular breastfeeding will remove any blocked milk from your breast, help to resolve the symptoms and also prevent mastitis from becoming more serious. In some cases, untreated mastitis can lead to infection. It's perfectly safe to breastfeed your baby when you have mastitis. Putting gel pads or cool cabbage leaves in your bra can bring some relief.

When to get help If your symptoms don't improve within 24 hours, see your doctor, as antibiotics may be required.

A soothing remedy For extreme discomfort, try placing cold, bruised cabbage leaves in your bra. The enzymes appear to reduce swelling and prevent over-supply of milk. They also work well to ease the pain of mastitis.

Looking after your breasts

Your breasts provide your baby's sole source of nutrition and hydration for the first six months of her life, so it's important that you look after them to keep you comfortable and encourage a good milk supply.

★ Always wear a supportive bra; your breasts need extra support when they're enlarged with milk. Wearing the correct bra can help to ease potential back pain and breast discomfort.

★ If your nipples become sore or cracked, first check that your baby is latched on correctly (see p.62). After feeding, rub a little breast milk around your nipples, which acts as an emollient, and leave your bra open for a while for your nipples to dry.

★ Use breast pads if your breasts tend to leak, as the moisture can cause them to become sore and irritated. Avoid using plastic-backed breast pads, and change any pads that become even a little damp.

★ Always use a breast pump correctly; some women find hand pumps difficult to operate and find it easier to use an electrical pump or to express by hand (see p.72).

★ Avoid using soap or any perfumed creams on your nipples. If they do become sore, use a lanolin-based cream or ointment that is suitable for breastfeeding.

★ Start feeds on the breast that is the least sore, and when your baby is finished feeding strongly, remove her.

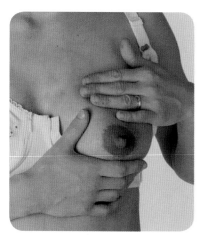

Relieving fullness If your breasts feel engorged, or you feel that there's a problem with flow, ensure that your baby is latched on well and that your breast is emptied. Massage your breast from the fullest part, down to the nipple, to move things along.

Helping your baby If she struggles to get a grip on an engorged breast, manually express a little milk first. Continue feeding from the engorged breast, which will offer relief. Try to relax when you're feeding, as this helps the milk flow more easily.

Successful breastfeeding

Once breastfeeding is established, there can be no better and easier way to feed your baby. Most mums report an intense closeness with their babies during feeding, which helps your baby to feel more secure.

When feeding goes well

The early days of feeding can be fraught with anxiety, but as your baby thrives, you'll be able to relax and enjoy the whole process.

Predictable routines It will become easier to distinguish between your baby's different cries, and play with him or simply give him a cuddle him when he needs something more than milk. Feeding times will be more predictable, and you should be able to establish some sort of a routine as your baby gains weight and begins naturally to establish his own pattern, usually from around four to six weeks.

Longer sleeps The engorged and uncomfortable feeling of the early days soon settles down, as your breasts adjust to producing just the right amount for your baby. Also, your baby will become a seasoned expert at feeding quickly and efficiently – often from both breasts at one sitting. You'll find, too, that he goes longer between feeds, which will mean a little more sleep for you.

Settling in Getting comfortable before a feed and relaxing for the duration makes the experience more positive, and helps your milk flow. Try not to worry about other things that need doing; instead, settle in and enjoy the experience of feeding your baby.

Well hydrated You can't underestimate the importance of staying hydrated while feeding. Drink a glass of water each time you feed your baby. Plenty of fluids help to keep you energized and help prevent problems such as blocked ducts and mastitis.

An additional supply Once feeding is established you can get into the habit of expressing milk and freezing it (see p.72), so that you can get out and about on your own when you feel that you need a break.

Public feeding Not all women feel comfortable feeding in public, but try to remember that it's a natural activity. There are now plenty of mother and baby rooms if you do want some privacy.

Feeding an older baby

There is plenty of research to suggest that breast milk continues to offer antibodies well into toddlerhood, which can help your little one to resist infection.

Essential nutrients Breast milk contains a readily absorbed form of iron, as well as protein, essential fatty acids, vitamins, minerals and enzymes, making it the perfect complement to a healthy, varied diet. Also, if your baby's diet is less than ideal once he has been weaned, breast milk may help to make up for any shortfalls.

Feeling close Most important, perhaps, breastfeeding offers emotional nourishment and comfort, and plays a strong role in a healthy mother-child relationship. The World Health Organisation suggests that breastfeeding should be continued for two years. This may seem a long time at this point, but it might be something you can aspire to.

TOP TIP

It's a good idea to avoid bottle feeds or dummies until breastfeeding is established to ensure that your baby doesn't experience "nipple confusion".

Extended breastfeeding There is no reason why breastfeeding can't continue for as long as you both enjoy it. Many mums feed for a year or more, and the benefits are clear for your baby's health, development and wellbeing.

Expressing milk

Many mums find that expressing gives them more freedom, as dad or a carer can help with feeding. If you're returning to work, expressing and storing a supply means that your baby still benefits from your breast milk.

Starting to express

There are no rights and wrongs, but consider these factors before starting to express your milk.

Get established first Milk production is based on supply and demand, so when your baby suckles, more milk is produced to meet her needs. If you express regularly, your milk will increase to ensure that the same quantity is available. It's a good idea to wait until your milk supply is established and your baby is feeding well and regularly, and putting on weight, before you start to express. Once your supply is established, you can begin to express and freeze or refrigerate your milk.

Wait a while Your baby may experience "nipple confusion" if you offer a bottle too early, and may want to be bottle-fed if she finds this easier. For this reason, it's best to wait until she is breastfeeding well before introducing her to a bottle.

Practise with a bottle Once you decide to give an occasional bottle, you'll have to teach your baby how to suck from it. You can try offering her a little water daily from a bottle first so that she gets used to the different way of feeding.

1 **Start manually expressing** by putting your hand about 2.5cm (an inch or so) back from your areola, and use your other fingers to cup your breast. Using your thumb and forefingers, press gently into your breast. Press and then release.

2 **Find a rhythm** that is comfortable for you, and, as you do so, imagine your baby. Rotate your hand around your areola, which can encourage your milk to flow. If nothing seems to work, try pressing a little further back from the nipple.

3 **Have a clean bowl** or sterilized bottle to collect the milk. Express each breast until the flow slows down – perhaps five minutes or so – then switch to the other side. You may wish to go back and forth a few times.

4 **Label your milk** with the date that it has been expressed before putting it in the freezer. It's important to ensure that the milk stays fresh, so as soon as it's labelled, store it in the fridge or freezer (see opposite).

Using an electric pump Place the breast cup or shield over your breast and turn on the machine. The pump will work to extract the milk from your breast into an attached container. It normally takes about 10–15 minutes to pump both breasts.

Using a manual pump As you would with the electric pump, place the cup or shield over your breast, with your nipple in the centre, then operate the squeeze mechanism or pull the plunger. It can take up to 45 minutes to express milk from both breasts.

Storing breast milk

It's reassuring to know that your breast milk can be kept in the fridge or freezer so that you can use it later.

What's its shelf life? You can store breast milk in the fridge for 24–48 hours. Put the milk in the coolest part of the fridge, at the back, not in the door. You can also store your milk for up to 14 days in the freezer compartment of the fridge, or for up to six months in a freezer at -18°C (0°F). Always store your milk in a sterilized container. Wash your pump well after using it, and sterilize it before using it again.

How do I use frozen milk? Defrost frozen breast milk in the fridge and then use it straightaway. Never refreeze your milk once it has thawed, and don't warm defrosted milk in the microwave.

Getting dad involved Your baby will enjoy getting close to dad as she feeds, and she'll be more likely to take a bottle with the familiar taste of your milk. If you plan to return to work, encourage your baby to take a bottle of expressed milk a few weeks before you return.

Extra care with milk As well as labelling your milk with the date when it was expressed and stored, make sure that you use it within the recommended time (see above).

Bottle-feeding basics

Formula offers your baby all of the essential nutrients he needs and is designed to be as close to breast milk as possible. Make bottle-feeding nurturing by feeding your baby skin-to-skin, or holding him close.

Which bottle? You will need at least six bottles. There's a huge variety available, including standard plastic types, anti-colic, disposable and self-sterilizing bottles, as well as glass bottles that are chemical-free.

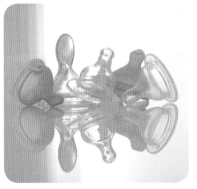

Teats Most teats are bought according to a baby's age. Teats can be latex or silicone and you need to decide on "flow"; the rate at which the milk comes out. Some babies like flatter teats that mimic the breast shape.

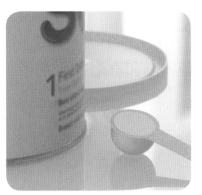

Formula Perfectly balanced to ensure that they are easily digestible, formula will meet your baby's needs for fluid and food. Follow the instructions exactly, and buy formula appropriate for your baby's age.

Bottle brushes Brushes that are specially designed to clean bottles and teats reach into all the crevices that could harbour traces of milk. Thorough cleaning is essential to prevent bacteria from breeding.

Sterilizers Your baby's bottles, and the equipment used to make up his milk, need to be sterilised using high heat, such as steam, or with cold-water treatments that are designed to kill any germs.

Going out A thermos flask (used only for this purpose) with boiled water and a sterilized plastic container with the required amount of formula are ideal for feeding when out. Mix a sterilized bottle when needed.

Giving a bottle Your baby will enjoy relaxing in your arms as you give him his bottle. Keep the bottle slightly tilted while you feed him so that the teat is filled with milk and he doesn't swallow extra air.

Choosing formula milk

Most infant formulas are derived from cow's milk, modified to resemble breast milk as closely as possible. There's little to choose between the big brands, but there are a few factors that you might like to consider.

Right balance of proteins Breast milk contains two types of protein: whey and casein. The balance in breast milk is 60 per cent whey, and 40 per cent casein. It's a good idea to choose a formula with a similar ratio. Formulas with a greater percentage of casein tend to be harder for your baby to digest, and there is some evidence that whey protein seems to provide more protection against infections.

Your baby's age Formula is designed and constituted to meet the needs of growing babies; what's appropriate for younger babies won't necessarily be right later on. First-stage milks are suitable from birth and contain all the nutrients your growing baby needs. Low-iron formulas are not suitable for most babies, who need good quantities of iron to grow and develop properly.

Bigger appetites Brands aimed at "hungrier" babies tend to have more casein, but unless your doctor or health visitor recommends these, normal formula will meet your baby's needs, and may be more appropriate for a young baby, whose immune system is not yet fully developed.

Bottle-feeding hygiene

Everything used to feed your baby and make up her formula needs to be scrupulously washed to remove all traces of milk, and then sterilized to kill any bacteria or other bugs that could harm your baby's health.

What you'll need

For washing bottles and equipment you will need:

★ A clean empty sink

★ Bottle and teat brush

★ Washing up liquid

For sterilizing the equipment you'll need:

★ A sterilizing system. This can be purpose made, such as a steam sterilizer, a microwave steamer or a cold sterilizing system (with tablets). Or you can use a saucepan used for boiling bottle-feeding equipment only.

1 **Discard any leftover milk.** It's important to not keep milk leftover from a previous feed because of the danger of bacteria developing. Rinse the bottle with cold water to remove any milk.

2 **Wash your baby's bottles and teats** in hot soapy water. Use a teat and bottle brush to remove every trace of milk. This is important, as milk is a breeding ground for bacteria.

TOP TIP

You can use the dishwasher to wash your baby's bottles, but you should sterilize them afterwards with a recommended sterilizing method.

3 **Turn the teat inside out** to clean off bits of milk that have been missed in the washing process. Squirt water through the holes to remove any milk residue.

4 **Rinse bottles and teats well** to ensure that you remove any soap or lingering milk that can trap bacteria. Soap residue can also affect the taste of formula, or upset your baby's tummy.

Microwave steaming This is similar to steaming in a sterilizing unit, and involves no boiling or chemicals. It takes 5–10 minutes, and you can keep equipment sterile in the unit for up to three hours.

Boiling Bottles, teats and equipment can be boiled in a lidded saucepan for five minutes. Cool the water, shake off excess, put the lids on bottles, and store everything in a clean, dry place. Repeated boiling can damage teats.

Cold-water sterilizing Follow the instructions, making up the solution in a glass or plastic container and ensuring there are no air pockets. You can leave everything in the solution until needed, but you should make up a fresh solution every 24 hours.

Steam sterilizers These are convenient and quick. Usually, a small amount of water is added to the base, and the bottles and teats are loaded. Always clean the unit as instructed. Sterilized items can often be left in the unit for up to 24 hours.

Making up a bottle

Your baby's bottle must be made up to the manufacturer's instructions to get the right balance of nutrients and liquid. Too much formula powder or liquid can cause your baby to become constipated, or thirsty; too little may mean that his bottle isn't meeting his nutritional needs.

Bottle-feeding guidelines

In the past, the advice was that bottles could be made up and stored in the fridge. Now this is known to cause tummy upsets and gastro-enteritis in some babies.

Making fresh feeds Milk powder isn't sterile, so even if you sterilize bottles, teats and equipment, there is a small risk that your baby's milk could become contaminated with microorganisms. For this reason, it is recommended that you make up a bottle as and when it is required.

Storing feeds When this isn't possible, store bottles in the fridge below 5°C (41°F). Prepared bottles are best kept in the back of the fridge. Check the fridge temperature regularly. Store bottles for no longer than 24 hours, less for very young babies. Never keep leftover feeds as bacteria can grow quickly in milk. When your baby has finished, throw away any leftovers.

Warming feeds You can warm the feed using a bottle warmer or by placing in a bowl of hot water; don't leave it warming for more than 15 minutes. Shake the bottle after heating, and test the temperature on the inside of your wrist.

1 **Pour cooled**, freshly boiled water into a sterilized bottle (avoid bottled spring or mineral water). Measure the formula, levelling scoops with a clean, sterilized knife, or the leveller on the carton.

2 **Add the formula** to the water. Make sure that you follow the manufacturer's instructions carefully and add the exact amount of formula required to the bottle.

3 **Shake your baby's bottle** very well before giving it to your baby, as formula powders and liquids have a tendency to stick to the sides of the teat. Once shaken, your baby's milk should have a creamy consistency and there should be no visible lumps.

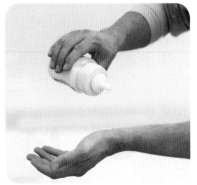

4 **If the bottle is made** with cool water, you may need to heat it in a jug of hot water. Always test the temperature of the milk on the inside of your wrist before feeding your baby. When it feels just warm to the touch, it's the right temperature for your baby.

Out and about

Bottle-feeding while on the go requires some planning. There are a few ways to transport your baby's milk.

Pre-mixed formulas These are expensive, but they can be carried with you, dispensed into a sterilized bottle and used on the spot, with no mixing or preparation.

Preparing away from home Boiling water can be put in a vacuum flask and used to make up fresh formula when required while out. In a sterilized plastic container, measure out the amount of powder required for one feed. Carry a sterilized bottle and add the water and formula when required, washing your hands before doing so. Take care that you don't scald yourself when making up the feed, and let the milk cool before feeding your baby.

Ready-mixed formula Remember to wash your hands before decanting a carton of ready-made formula into a bottle. If the carton is dusty, wipe or wash it and then use clean scissors to open it.

Transporting feeds If you do take a made-up bottle with you, put it in an insulated bag or bottle carrier that keeps it cold to avoid bacteria breeding. Better still, use the methods, right, to bottle-feed while you're out.

Giving your baby a bottle

Make the experience of being fed pleasurable and nurturing by holding your baby close. Keep her pressed close to your chest, so that she can hear your heartbeat, smell you and feel comforted.

Which teat?

There is a huge number of teats now available, and all have various merits. Think about what suits both you and your baby's needs.

Latex teats Their softness can make it easier for babies to suck (particularly if they tend to be weak suckers).

Silicone teats These are generally more expensive and are less flexible than latex, but last longer.

Size and flow Buy teats that are the right size for the age of your baby, and experiment a bit to see if she prefers fast or slow-flow teats. Teats with a wide, flat base and a nipple-shaped centre appeal to some babies, particularly those who have been breastfed, or fed in both ways.

1 **Start by stroking your baby's cheek,** looking into her eyes and talking to her. Skin-to-skin contact is recommended to mimic breastfeeding.

2 **Hold the teat to her lips** so she will open her mouth. Tilt the bottle so that the formula fills the neck of the bottle and covers the teat.

3 **Don't encourage your baby to finish** the bottle if she's not interested. To remove the bottle from your baby, place your clean little finger in your baby's mouth to break the suction.

Helping with bottles The whole family can get involved when giving bottles of expressed breast milk or formula. Older siblings may like to help feed their new little brother or sister, but be sure that you sit alongside, keep a firm grip on your baby, and supervise.

Winding your baby

You need to wind your baby to prevent air getting trapped in her digestive system. All babies need to be winded after a feed, and sometimes during one. However, bottlefed babies tend to require special attention, as the action of sucking from a bottle rather than the breast means that they take in more air.

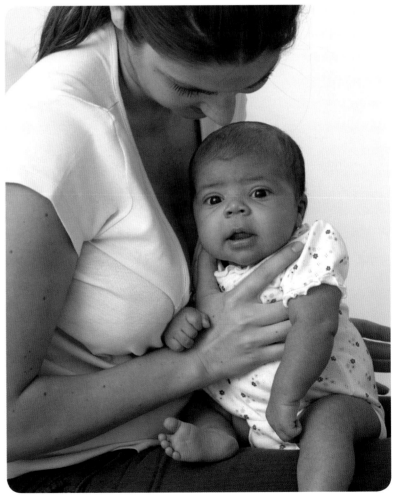

Over your shoulder Support your baby's head if his neck muscles aren't strong while you hold him over your shoulder. Gently rub or pat his back until he burps. It's common for babies to bring up a little milk when they burp, so you might want to protect your shoulder with a muslin or a towel first. It's sometimes possible to feel an air bubble working its way up your baby's body and out.

TOP TIP

Many types of formula are available to help babies who suffer with wind or reflux. The formulas for reflux are usually thicker and you may need to use a teat with a larger hole.

Sitting position While you are in a sitting position, seat your baby on your lap, with one hand on her chest, supporting her chin, and the other on her back. Gently lean her forward, and rub or gently pat her back until she brings up some air. It may take some time for bubbles to emerge, so be patient.

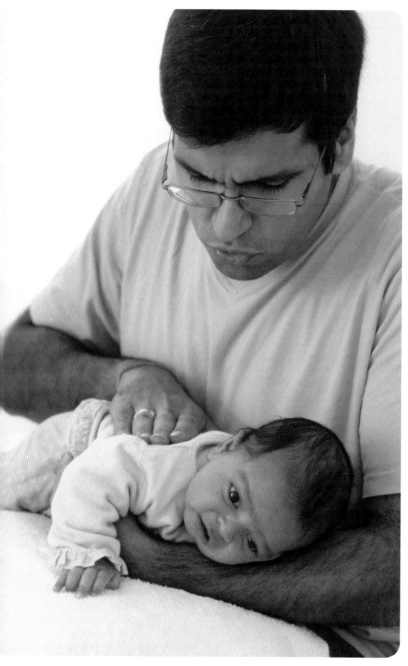

Face down Place your baby face down on your lap, with your hand and forearm supporting her head and chin. Keep her slightly upright, so that the air bubbles can travel upwards more easily. Rub or gently pat her back. You should avoid this method if your baby shows any signs of reflux.

Possetting and reflux

Possetting happens when your baby regurgitates a small amount of milk after feeds, and it's completely normal. Reflux is a more severe form of possetting and may need investigating.

How to minimize possetting In most cases, possetting occurs when air bubbles become trapped while feeding. Normal winding, halfway through, and at the end of a feed usually bring these up, but a small amount of milk may reappear too.

You can reduce possetting by handling your baby gently after a feed, especially when winding. Support him upright for up to 20 minutes after a feed, and provide smaller, more frequent feeds. Changing your baby's nappy before a feed to avoid laying him down afterwards can help, too.

When reflux is a problem A more severe form of possetting, reflux usually results from a weak or immature valve that lies between the oesophagus (the tube leading from your baby's throat to his tummy) and the tummy.

In almost all cases, reflux resolves itself by 18 months, and doesn't harm your baby. However, if your baby brings up a large percentage of his feed, is not putting on weight, seems listless, tired or distressed by the vomiting, there may be another cause, so talk to your doctor. Severe reflux can be painful, and you may need advice about special formulas that "stay down"; changing the teat to a slower-flowing one; or, in extreme cases, using a prescription antacid designed for babies.

Bottle-feeding problems

Some babies struggle with bottle-feeding, and it can take trial and error to get the formula, teat, feeding position and winding right. Most problems are easily dealt with and your baby will settle down within a couple of weeks.

Bottle-feeding tips

Follow these tips to ensure that bottle-feeding runs smoothly.

★ Some babies are sensitive to a change in formula, so keep plenty on hand, along with some pre-mixed cartons of the same brand in case of emergencies.

★ Don't be tempted to add cereal or anything else to your baby's milk. If she is constantly hungry, try feeding her more often; however, if she is putting on weight too quickly, or not quickly enough, see your doctor. Your baby should stay on roughly the same centile line on her growth charts (see p.59) as she grows and develops.

★ For older babies, a routine can help, as your baby knows what to expect and begins to look forward to feeding as a positive, regular experience. That said, it is important to be flexible and feed your baby when she is hungry, to ensure that she is getting what she needs when she needs it.

★ If your baby suffers from excessive wind, try using an anti-colic bottle, as there's evidence that these reduce wind.

★ Babies love to be cuddled and held, and any interaction you have with your baby during this time will encourage the bonding process.

★ Enjoy the experience. Get close to your baby – try skin-to-skin, just as you would if you were breastfeeding – and get the bonding going!

Cause for concern Some babies fail to digest the lactose or proteins in milk, are uncomfortable after feeds and fail to thrive. If your baby is uncomfortable after winding, talk to your doctor about possible causes.

Excessive possetting Most babies bring up a little milk in the early months, which is normal. However, if your baby regularly vomits and seems to be in pain when she is fed, see your doctor or health visitor.

Fluid intake If your baby has less than five wet nappies a day, and/or his faeces are hard, she may not be getting enough fluid. Check that feeds are made up correctly, feed her regularly and give cooled, boiled water.

Check the flow If your baby struggles when feeding, check the teat flow. If it takes longer than 20 minutes to finish a bottle, switch to a faster teat. If she chokes or splutters, the flow may be too fast.

When to wind Babies who tend to suffer from trapped air bubbles will often benefit from being winded mid-feed, and held upright as soon as they have finished the bottle. Hold him gently and rub or pat his back. If nothing else, he'll feel comforted by the close contact with you.

Is my baby getting enough milk?

It's normal to worry that your baby isn't getting enough milk, especially if she takes very little at a feed, or seems particularly hungry. But rest assured that infant appetites are very variable and, if she's growing normally, she's sure to be getting what she needs.

How many feeds? Newborns have six to eight feeds per day, dropping to four or five by the time they hit seven months. The amount you offer should be based on your baby's weight, and she should be satisfied by the time she finishes her bottle.

Look at the overall pattern
Sometimes your baby will be thirstier because it's hot, at other times she might feed greedily because she's going through a growth spurt, or she might not seem interested in finishing her feed at all. Rather than look at what she's taking at each individual feed, look at the bigger picture. If her growth rate is normal and she's healthy and alert, she's getting the right amount.

Listen to his cues If your baby has lost interest in her bottle, stop feeding her; she needs to learn to recognize her "full" cue, and she should not be fed past this point.

Ask for advice If you are worried that your baby isn't thriving, talk to your health visitor or doctor. Don't set your own quantities of formula.

Weaning your baby

It is recommended that babies are exclusively breastfed for the first six months, after which you can start introducing solid foods. He will still need his usual breast milk or formula but will gradually expand his diet.

Starting on solids

From six months, if your baby is hungry at the end of a feed, wakes early for feeds, and starts waking again in the night, he is ready for solids. The guidelines here will help you get started.

★ Feed your baby in his highchair at the kitchen table and eat together. This introduces your baby to the concept of sociable mealtimes, encourages an interest in food and helps him develop good table manners through your example. In addition, family mealtimes help his language development.

★ Introduce solids first at lunchtime, as new foods can unsettle him, and this will be easier to deal with during the day.

★ Encourage your baby to self-feed (see p.96).

★ Build up to giving your baby about one large cup of food per meal, the equivalent of an 250ml (8oz) milk feed. By the time he is 12 months old, he will probably be on three meals and two milk feeds a day. Although milk remains the mainstay of his diet for the first year, you can gradually reduce the amount of milk he has as his food intake grows.

★ Don't introduce solids when your baby is unwell with a cold or a rash.

★ If your baby refuses a food, leave it for the moment, then offer it again at a later meal. It can take several attempts for a food to be accepted.

★ Never force a food on your baby, or offer bribes or distractions.

Sitting comfortably Well before your baby is ready for weaning, he should be able sit confidently upright and hold his neck and head up. Babies should be fed in an upright position, not in a reclining seat, to encourage healthy digestion and prevent choking.

Can I eat it? Putting everything into his mouth suggests your baby is ready for non-milk foods. But he needs to lose his tongue-thrust reflex (which pushes food out and so protects him from choking) before he can master chewing and swallowing.

Your hungry baby Your baby may become unsatisfied after milk feeds and wake at night hungry, having previously slept through. However, most babies have a growth spurt at this time, so she may be hungry for this reason, rather than being ready for solids.

I want some too Your baby may reach out for the food on your plate. She may show interest when you eat, and watch the whole process with amazement. She may actually salivate when you eat, and make chewing motions with her mouth.

Weaning myths

There are many grandparents who insist that babies should be weaned from as early as two or three months! This may have been advised years ago, but not any more. Learn to sort fact from fiction when it comes to the subject of weaning …

Myth: Babies need teeth to be weaned. Some babies cut their first teeth well before the 17-week mark, and others don't get any until they approach their first birthday. Weaning is unrelated to teething – you'll be amazed at what babies can do with a little creative gumming.

Myth: Solids help babies sleep for longer. Early weaning can actually disrupt sleep, because your baby's digestive system has not developed enough to cope with solid food, causing discomfort. If your baby is always waking at night, chances are he has not learned how to settle himself to sleep.

Myth: Solids will help babies to put on weight. Most babies will be a healthy weight as a result of milk alone. Furthermore, when you introduce your baby to solid foods, you are not adding many calories – or indeed fat – which would encourage weight gain, as first foods are based around fruit, vegetables and gluten-free grains. Underweight babies may have trouble feeding, and it's worth seeing your doctor to establish why.

Weaning equipment

Making fresh, healthy food for your baby is a great way to introduce her to solids and ensure that she gets the right nutrients. Getting equipped with a few basics can make the process easier – and more rewarding.

Your baby's highchair You should sit your baby in a highchair as soon as you start to wean him. By six months, he is developmentally ready to sit up, either unsupported, or you can insert a couple of cushions at first for extra support.

Making purées If you're making purées, use a hand blender, a food processor or a food grinder (mouli) to whiz up fruit and vegetable purées for your baby. Purées such as ripe peach, papaya and banana are easy to prepare as they don't need cooking.

Storing prepared food It's a good idea to have cube trays or small containers to batch cook food and freeze baby-sized portions of purpose-made purées or mashed up meals. Cover the trays or pots to preserve nutrients. Freeze at -18°C or below within 24 hours.

Containing the mess Babies are extremely messy while they learn the art of eating. A soft, washable bib protects clothing, and acts as a napkin if she gets messy. When she's a bit older, try a soft plastic or rubber bib with a turned-up "trough" at the base.

Splash mats These are designed to fit under your baby's highchair and catch the inevitable mess made during mealtimes, saving you endless floor mopping. Choose sturdy, wipe-clean designs that can be easily folded away and stored when not in use.

Weaning utensils There's a huge variety of weaning equipment, with travel bowl and spoon sets, bowls with a suction cup and easily held cutlery and beakers. First weaning spoons should have a narrow head and shallow bowl to help your baby suck off food.

A new perspective Get your baby used to sitting in a highchair as early as possible. Choose a chair with a five-point safety harness. Padded inserts ensure that she sits snugly, and removable trays that can be carried to the bin and the sink are useful.

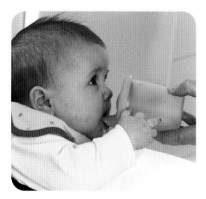

Your baby's first cup Now is a good time to introduce your baby to a beaker. Water can accompany her meals, but milk remains the mainstay of her diet. Choose a non-spill beaker so she can experiment without losing its contents!

At the table When your baby is a bit older, he can sit at the table with a sturdy clip-on chair, or simply remove his highchair tray and push him up to the table. Your baby will enjoy sociable mealtimes and is more likely to try new things if he feels part of the gang.

Continuing with milk feeds

A common misconception is that the beginning of weaning marks the end of breast- or bottle-feeding, but this could not be further from the truth.

New tastes Your baby will continue to get the majority of her nutrients from his regular milk for many months to come. The process of weaning begins simply with an introduction to food, which involves offering her tastes of a variety of different fruits, vegetables and gluten-free grains. The aim is to get your baby used to the idea of new tastes, but these do not become the mainstay of her diet.

Regular milk feeds For the first month or so of weaning, her milk feeds should continue as usual. You may want to offer her "meals" halfway through a feed, or after her morning sleep, which is usually around lunchtime.

Reducing milk feeds After a few weeks (or at six months), she can move on to a wider range of foods, including dairy produce, grains, meat, fish and eggs. As she progresses from first tastes towards regular meals, you can slowly reduce the number of feeds, or the length of time and/or amount you feed her. Again, don't give up her milk. Until they are a year old, babies need at least 500–600ml (1 pint) of formula or breast milk per day, and that means regular feeds.

89

First foods

Your baby's first non-milk foods accustom him to different textures and tastes, and encourage him to develop the skills needed to chew (or gum) foods and swallow. Take your time and enjoy the process together.

Kitchen hygiene

When preparing food for your baby, it's important to be very meticulous about hygiene. Follow the guidelines below:

★ Always wash your hands before preparing any food for your baby.

★ Freeze food within 24 hours of preparing, and defrost it thoroughly before reheating.

★ When reheating previously prepared food, ensure that it is thoroughly heated through, then allow it to cool. Avoid reheating food in a microwave and don't reheat food a second time.

★ Throw away food left over in your baby's bowl, and any uneaten food that has been in contact with his saliva.

★ Ensure that kitchen surfaces and chopping boards are scrupulously clean. Clean your baby's highchair before and after meals, and keep the floor clean.

★ Take particular care that meat and eggs are thoroughly cooked through.

TOP TIP

If you start off with purées, it's a good idea to increase your baby's confidence with an increasing number of tastes and textures to help prevent him becoming a fussy eater.

1 **Prepare fruits and vegetables** for your baby by first peeling the skin. For an apple purée, chop the fruit into chunks and remove the core and hard ends. If you wish to give your baby some uncooked fruit, cut it into easily held segments.

2 **For an apple purée,** put the apple in a saucepan with a sprinkling of water, and then heat gently until the apple is reduced to a soft consistency. Don't add sugar to the purée. This is handy cooked in bulk to use for family desserts.

3 **Hand blenders** are ideal for purées. They are quick and easy to use and useful for your baby's first foods. As your baby gets used to new tastes, start to change the consistency of his purées by blending less to give a lumpier texture.

1 **Sit your baby in her highchair** when she's alert and interested. Scoop up some purée on the weaning spoon and, coming from the side, put the spoon to her lips. Don't force the spoon into her mouth – if she opens her mouth, gently insert the spoon.

2 **At first your baby will simply suck the food** from the spoon, rather than use her lips to remove the food. Allow her plenty of time to get used to the new sensation of having a spoon in her mouth and to work out how to use her mouth to remove the food.

3 **Hold the spoon in your baby's mouth** until she has sucked off its contents. If she doesn't do this at first, gently scrape the spoon against her upper gums so that the purée is left in her mouth, and then gently remove the spoon.

4 **You will know when she's had enough** so don't coerce her if she's lost interest or turns her head away. Most babies have only one or two spoonfuls at first – simply go at your baby's pace and you won't risk putting her off.

Baby-led weaning

There's growing interest in baby-led weaning, which involves skipping purées and encouraging your baby to feed herself. Nutritious foods are chopped, grated or cut up so that your baby's fingers can manage them.

Enjoying food There's evidence that babies weaned this way find the transition to lumpy foods easier and, because they're encouraged to chew from the outset, manage family meals earlier. Also, because they are given more choice, it's believed that they enjoy the process of eating more than traditionally weaned babies, and are less likely to be fussy eaters. Encourage your baby's involvement by passing food from your hand to his, squidging it between your fingers so he can lick it off.

Good starter foods These include potato wedges, lightly steamed cauliflower or broccoli, fresh avocado, banana or soft pears. Some babies play with the food or gnaw or suck on it. However, gradually, as he becomes used to the taste and the texture, he will begin to eat more – particularly when his milk feeds are reduced.

Supervision Watch him during meals, as most babies gag when they learn to chew and swallow. Have a feeding cup with water to hand. When he's finished, check he hasn't "stored" food in his cheeks. Lastly, even though he is feeding on his own, make sure you introduce foods at the appropriate stage (see p.92).

91

Introducing new foods

Your baby's first tastes should be offered when she is calm and alert. Don't be surprised if things don't go to plan. After six months of being held for feeds, a hard spoon with unfamiliar contents can be a surprise.

Which foods when?

The following is a guide to introducing your baby to new tastes and textures.

★ Most babies start with simple fruit and vegetable purées, as well as a little non-gluten cereal, such as baby rice.

★ Try foods one at a time at the outset, and then, when foods have been successfully introduced, you can offer a blend of fruit and vegetables. The more tastes you introduce, and the wider the range of combinations, the more likely she is to develop her palate and enjoy different foods.

★ From six months, fish, well-cooked eggs, dairy produce (although not cow's milk as a drink), meat, poultry, gluten grains (such as wheat), pulses (such as chickpeas and lentils), and nut butters can be introduced. If you make purées, these can begin to be slightly lumpier as you introduce your baby to increasingly textured food. Grate, finely chop and mash her food, blending it with purées to make it easier for her to manage.

★ From eight or nine months, your baby can now try a wider variety of foods and continue to eat home-cooked family foods that have been prepared so that they do not contain added salt and sugar.

★ You can begin to chop things less finely, and encourage her to try bigger chunks and lumps, which will require more chewing.

Early textures First tastes may be given as semi-liquid purées, which your baby can suck off the spoon. Once she's mastered a variety of foods in this form, begin to offer slightly lumpier purées.

Make it sociable Talk to your baby as you offer him his first tastes, and open your own mouth to show him what to do. Take a taste yourself to show that the food is delicious. Most babies are mimics and follow your lead.

Having fun Let her play with her food and explore textures. Although messy, it's part of the developmental process involved in learning to eat. She may dip her fingers in and suck them, or try to scoop up her food.

Mixing foods Start your baby on purées with single fruits and vegetables. Once she has a good repertoire, start to mix them. There's no reason why you can't mix fruits and vegetables, if that's what she enjoys.

Finger foods

These are ideal first foods, because they help your baby to develop the skills necessary to feed herself, and also persuade her to chew and to explore new tastes and textures at her own speed.

What to offer It's important not to offer foods that may cause your baby to choke, or that aren't appropriate for her age. Good first finger foods include avocado, pears, mango, papaya, and lightly cooked broccoli and green beans. Slivers of cheese, cooked potato and chicken are also fine. Remember to cut food into small pieces, removing skin or bones, and to lightly steam or boil hard vegetables to soften them before giving them to your baby.

A healthy selection Offer nutritious foods and stay close by your baby as she sucks and chews in case she chokes.

Foods to avoid in the first year

Your baby will begin to eat an increasing variety of foods as she becomes more adept; however, there are a few things that should remain off the menu until she's at least a year old:

★ **Undercooked eggs,** which can contain salmonella. Eggs should be well cooked until your child is at least 12 months old.

★ **Honey** is not recommended for babies under 12 months because there is a small risk of botulism, a bacterial type of food poisoning.

★ **Unpasteurized dairy products and runny cheeses,** which can cause bacterial infection.

★ **Low-fat dairy products** – your baby needs healthy fats for optimum growth and development.

★ **Artificial sweeteners, flavours and other additives and preservatives.** This means that processed foods are off the menu, as they have chemicals that could potentially harm your baby's health.

★ **Salt.** Don't add any salt to your baby's food. Use mashed up family foods and don't add salt when you cook.

★ **Sugar** can not only damage her teeth, but causes her to develop a sweet tooth that can lead to obesity. Sugar is empty calories, and when your baby is small, her food needs to be nutrient-dense.

★ **Nitrates,** which are found in processed meat and other foods, including some vegetables. You may choose organically grown vegetables to avoid high levels of nitrates, and avoid processed foods.

★ **Whole nuts,** which can cause choking. Nut butters and ground nuts can be offered from six months.

Your baby's healthy diet

Although milk provides most of your baby's nutrients for the first year, it's important to choose the healthiest foods and drinks for him. His tummy is small, and every mouthful should add to his nutrient intake. Like adults, he needs a balanced diet, even when he is eating only one or two meals a day.

The best drinks

As your baby progresses through the weaning process, he will take in less of his usual milk, which means that he'll need other drinks to keep him hydrated.

Milk Offer his usual milk in a cup at mealtimes. Cow's milk should not be given as a drink until he is at least 12 months old.

Water This is the ideal drink for babies. It keeps them hydrated and encourages digestion, and your baby will learn to enjoy the taste. It's the only drink that should be given between meals, as juice can damage teeth when not served with food.

Diluted fruit and vegetable juices These should be heavily watered down and served only with meals or snacks, as offering them at other times can lead to tooth decay. Juices do offer vitamins and minerals (including vitamin C, which is necessary for iron to be absorbed).

Drinks between meals If your baby is thirsty between meals, offer small sips of water first rather than a milk feed; if he's still unhappy, give a little of his usual milk.

Drinking on a full stomach Your baby's tummy is small and drinks fill him up, preventing him from getting enough food to provide the nutrients he needs. It's a good idea therefore to offer drinks towards the end of a meal.

A balanced diet

Your baby will begin with only a few tastes at each mealtime. By seven months, he should be eating three small meals a day, with food from each of the food groups below. Until he is a year old, he still needs about 600ml (1 pint) of breast milk or formula, but he will get this in fewer feeds.

Overall nutrition Don't worry too much if your baby doesn't get a little of every food group in each sitting. It's more important to look at the overall picture – as long as he is getting a few servings of everything across the day, he'll be doing well. As he heads towards two or three full meals a day, make sure that he gets at least a spoonful of fruit and vegetables, a carbohydrate (such as pasta, potato or baby rice), some protein (in the form of some lentils, soya, meat, fish, dairy produce) and some healthy fats, also contained in dairy produce, eggs, nut butters, ground seeds and meat. Variety is more important than quantity.

Carbohydrates These provide the energy to grow and develop. Complex carbohydrates, which are unrefined, such as wholegrain cereals, breads, brown rice and pasta, and fruit and vegetables are the healthiest carbohydrates for your baby and will provide him with plenty of fibre, a little protein, as well as vitamins and minerals. Most importantly, they provide a sustained source of energy.

Fats These are essential for babies, and required for many body functions, including the nervous system. More than 50 per cent of the calories in breastmilk come from fat, of which the most important type is EFAs, or essential fatty acids. These are found in oily fish, nuts, seeds, vegetable oils and avocados, as well as some grains, such as quinoa. These are important for growth, development, behaviour and the ability to learn. Avoid hydrogenated trans fats. Saturated fats, which are found in full-fat dairy produce and meat, have been linked with health problems, such as cardiovascular disease; however, your baby does need them in small quantities.

Proteins Fish, lean meats, pulses (such as lentils, beans, peas and chickpeas), soya, dairy produce, eggs, wholegrains and chicken, all contain protein, which provides your baby's body with the tools he needs to grow and develop. He'll need several servings of good-quality protein each day.

Fibre This is found in fruit, vegetables and wholegrains, and it has a host of roles in your baby's body, including ensuring healthy digestion and bowel movements, stimulating saliva to protect his teeth, and encouraging the uptake of nutrients from the food your baby eats.

Vitamins and minerals Your baby needs all the vitamins and minerals found in a balanced diet that includes protein, complex carbohydrates, good-quality fats and lots of fresh fruit and vegetables.

Iron is especially important for your baby's development and growth. This key mineral is found in dried fruits, meat, leafy-green vegetables, pulses and iron-fortified cereals. Also important is vitamin C, found in most fruits and vegetables. This is required for your baby's overall health and, in particular, his immune system, bones and skin. It's also necessary for iron to be absorbed.

Vitamin D, needed for bones and teeth, is in eggs, oily fish and dairy produce.

Finally, your baby needs calcium for healthy bones and teeth, and other body functions. This is found in leafy green vegetables, dairy produce, sesame seeds, almond and soya.

Every other vitamin and mineral is required, too, so ensure that your baby's diet is balanced.

Complex carbohydrates Wholemeal bread is a good start to your baby's day.

Avocado This is an ideal first food: soft, full of vitamins, and containing healthy fats.

Oily fish These contain essential fatty acids and calcium. Take care with bones.

Fresh fruit and veg These have vitamins and minerals and aid iron absorption.

Avoiding feeding pitfalls

If you experience setbacks when your baby is teething or under the weather, or she is ravenously hungry before a growth spurt or developmental leap, go at your baby's pace and keep mealtimes pleasurable and relaxed.

Fussy eaters

Some babies appear to be fussy eaters from the outset, and others develop this particular habit when they realise that they will get attention. There are a few ways to avoid this problem.

★ **Begin weaning with vegetables**, which aren't quite as sweet as fruit. Babies who begin with fruit tend to resist anything more savoury, and can develop a sweet tooth.

★ **Always start a meal with a savoury purée** and then move on to fruit. Babies will usually reject the savouries if you do it the other way round.

★ **Continue to offer the same food at different sittings** until it becomes familiar. Research shows that it can take up to 10 tries for your baby to accept it.

★ **Don't fall into the trap** of offering the same foods over and again with no break. If your baby won't eat something new, calmly remove it and try again another day. If she is hungry, she will eat; rest assured, she won't starve!

★ **Don't react when she takes a stand.** Some babies like to get a reaction from mum or dad, and will make a fuss for that reason.

★ **Share your food** when you are eating, and make it clear that you are enjoying it very much. She'll probably be intrigued enough to try it herself.

Let her join in Give your baby her own, chunky, baby-sized spoon and perhaps her own bowl. She'll feel in control of the process, which will satisfy a growing independent streak. You'll need to feed her too, to ensure that some food goes in.

Take it slowly If your baby is reluctant to take food from a spoon, ease him into the process. Offer a little purée on a clean finger for him to taste and then suck off. Encourage him to do the same.

A broader repertoire Some babies have favourites, and refuse new foods at first. Try mixing a favourite purée with something new. If your baby closes his mouth, this can also mean "I want to do it myself".

Sociable mealtimes Whenever possible, feed your baby at the family table. Not only will she learn table manners and understand the process of eating, but she will be inspired to try new things. Let her reach out and try appropriate foods, and try to give her the same or a similar meal, so that she feels involved.

Regular mealtimes

Babies are creatures of routine and habit, and enjoy knowing what to expect – and when.

Daily schedule Try to offer your baby meals at roughly the same time every day, so that she can begin to anticipate them with pleasure. In the early days, you may wish to give her a little of her usual milk, to take the edge off her hunger and create a sense of calm and wellbeing.

Eating together Later on, she can eat at family mealtimes, and join in with the fun. At the outset, it doesn't matter how much food she eats; the trick is to encourage her to try new foods, and develop a varied diet – and palate!

Watch and learn If she refuses to eat, let her sit with the family and simply watch. Chances are she will want to be involved sooner or later.

Feeling secure Some babies feel lonely in a highchair. If so, put him on your lap for his first tastes, holding him close. Once he's used to the idea of a spoon and new tastes, graduate to the highchair. Or introduce him to his highchair before weaning, giving him toys or little pots of water to play with.

Follow her cue If your baby is unhappy, end the meal; there's no point in forcing her to eat. If she develops negative associations about food, or realizes that she can provoke a strong reaction from you by resisting, you will set yourself up for trouble later! Calmly remove and comfort her, and try again later.

TOP TIP
Try to avoid feeding your baby when she's feeling overtired, cranky or very hungry. She'll want one thing only – milk – and she may resist attempts to sit her in a highchair.

Food allergies and intolerances

A small number of babies may be allergic to or intolerant of certain foods, such as soya, wheat, eggs, nuts, seeds, peanuts, fish and shellfish. Be aware of the symptoms and watch your baby closely.

Symptoms of an allergy or intolerance

It's worth noting that many symptoms of allergies can be perfectly normal in healthy children, so don't panic. Report your concerns to your doctor, and keep a food diary to work out if they are repeated when the food is introduced again. Your baby may also temporarily experience symptoms if he is unwell. The following are possible symptoms of an allergy or intolerance.

★ A rash or hives around the mouth, lips and eyes

★ Facial swelling

★ A runny nose

★ Vomiting or diarrhoea (particularly if it contains mucus)

★ Eczema

★ Tummy pain or cramping

★ Frequent distress or crying

★ Wheezing

★ If your baby experiences breathing problems, or becomes suddenly pale, inexplicably sleepy, floppy, confused or loses consciousness, call an ambulance immediately. This type of reaction is known as anaphylaxis and it is life-threatening, as your baby is effectively going into shock.

Keep a food diary Watch for allergy and intolerance with a food diary, noting down reactions to new foods. Introduce foods one at a time; leave a day or so between foods to give time to assess possible symptoms.

Check the ingredients If you aren't sure what might have caused the problems, check ingredients on any packaging. If a food allergy is diagnosed, you will need to become adept at reading labels.

Delayed reactions If your baby seems uncomfortable with vomiting, diarrhoea or cramping, consider what she has eaten in the last 24–48 hours. Some allergies don't appear until the second or third tasting.

Tell-tale rash A rash around the mouth after eating is a classic sign of food allergy, and you may notice hives (raised, red or pale bumps) on his skin. This type of reaction tends to be fairly instantaneous.

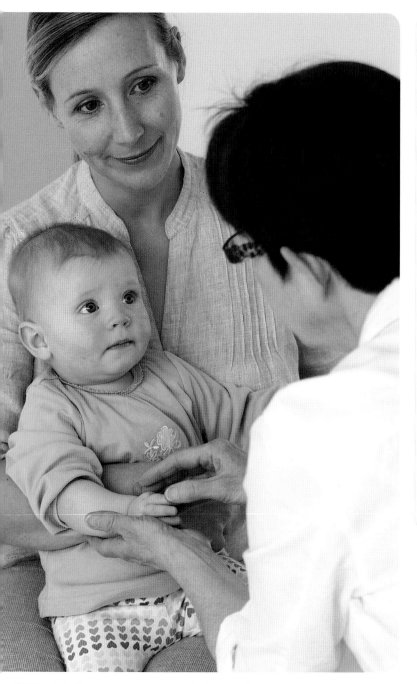

Getting help If you have concerns, your doctor can refer you to an allergy specialist, who uses a series of tests to diagnose allergies, and can provide support from a nutritionist to ensure that your baby's diet remains balanced.

Living with allergies

It is possible for your allergic baby to have a healthy, balanced diet, and to grow and develop normally.

Be vigilant You will need to take every precaution to avoid your baby being accidentally contaminated by the offending food. Read food labels carefully. Labelling has improved dramatically over the years and should now indicate whether any of the major allergens are present.

Look for alternatives Once an allergy is diagnosed, a nutritionist will help you find alternative foods. For example, if your baby is allergic to dairy, you'll need to find other forms of calcium. If he is allergic to wheat, you may need to replace gluten-containing grains with gluten-free ones, such as corn or rice.

Make carers aware Tell everyone who cares for your baby about his allergies, and what to do in an emergency. Some parents will need to carry injectors in the event of an anaphylactic reaction, or at least an antihistamine to relieve symptoms.

KEY FACT
Allergies occur when the immune system reacts to harmless proteins. Often, babies can be intolerant of foods after an illness. Wait until they're well, then try to offer the food again.

Your baby's sleep

SLEEP AND YOUR BABY

There are few issues that trouble new parents more than their baby's sleep habits – or lack of them! Young babies wake often in the night to feed, and can find it hard to settle back to sleep. Over time, though, most babies do start to sleep through.

New parenting can be exhausting. Getting to grips with your baby's needs, feeding, changing and simply working out the best ways to settle him can all be draining in themselves. On top of all this, you also have to deal with your baby's erratic sleep patterns, which means being woken up frequently during the night.

The good news is that there are a number of ways to establish healthy sleep patterns early on, and encourage your baby to sleep soundly and regularly. Sleep is as important for your baby as it is for you, and if you get enough, you'll undoubtedly feel more energetic and optimistic, as well as calmer. The secret to getting enough sleep yourself is, of course, through ensuring that your

baby sleeps well, too! While in the early weeks it's best to accept that you will have broken nights, over time you can try to establish a regular bedtime routine and good sleep habits that will encourage your baby to sleep through the night.

YOUR BABY'S NEEDS
Newborn babies have tiny tummies and need to feed regularly throughout the day and the night, particularly in the early days. Some parents claim that their babies slept through the night from the outset; this is not only unusual, but not particularly healthy, either. Up until six months, all babies continue to need night feeds according to their size. After a few weeks, you can start

to help your baby distinguish night from day and, if he is growing normally, he'll be able to settle for slightly longer periods at night.

As a very general guide, a one-month-old baby's tummy can hold enough milk (85–115ml/3–4floz) to sustain a three to four hour sleep at night; by three months, this may extend to about five hours; by five months to around seven hours; and by six months, when your baby can take up to 230ml (8floz) milk, he is capable of sleeping for up to eight hours – though he may well not! Remember that if you're breastfeeding, although you can't measure your baby's milk intake, your body will produce the right amount for his needs.

YOUR BABY'S COMFORT
It's important always to check that your baby is comfortable before you try to settle him. Has he been winded, is his nappy clean and not too tight and does he have enough blankets to keep him cosy without overheating? You also need to be aware of, and address any feeding difficulties that may affect his ability to settle, such as reflux (see p.83); or poor latching on (see p.68), which can affect how much milk he gets, in turn making him less settled.

HELPING YOUR BABY TO SLEEP
Getting your baby to settle himself is the source of much parental anxiety in the early weeks and months. However, it's helpful to know that most sleep problems are caused by incorrect sleep associations. For example, if, after six weeks, you continue to give your baby a feed as soon as he wakes without first checking if there's another reason for him waking, he'll continue to expect this, even when he no longer needs a feed.

When helping your baby to settle, it helps to bear in mind the principles of good sleep. One is establishing your baby's body clock. After about six weeks, if your baby is gaining weight at the expected rate, you can start to try develop a more regular pattern of feeding and sleeping (based on the loose guidelines above as to how much milk his

Side by side Keeping your baby close for the first six months is recommended and enables you to attend to him easily at night.

Random sleeps In the early weeks, babies sleep whenever they need to, usually taking short mini-sleeps rather than long snoozes.

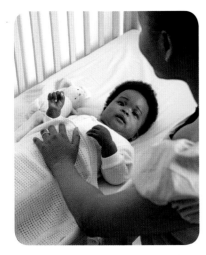

Settling down When your baby is tired but not quite ready to settle, it can help to pat and soothe him until he's really sleepy.

tummy can hold) and encourage him to sleep for longer at night with more wakeful periods in the day.

Another principle is to set good sleep associations early on. If you regularly rock, pat or nurse your baby until he is asleep and then put him into his cot, for example, he is not able to practise going to sleep without you. There is much debate about the right way to settle babies to sleep. There are those who advocate "controlled crying" and sleep training methods and those who prefer a gentler approach, where they don't leave their baby to cry (see pp.118–119). But no matter what your parenting style, the general consensus is that you need to put your baby down when he is just awake enough to realize that he is in his cot, on his own (even if you don't actually leave him). He can then learn to drift off without needing you to send him off to sleep.

DEALING WITH PROBLEMS

Even when you do establish a routine and your baby begins to sleep longer and to a regular pattern, things can go awry at times and your baby may begin to wake again in the night after previously sleeping through, or wake regularly at the crack of dawn. At key stages of development (when he learns to roll, for example, or sit or crawl), he may wake more often to try out his new tricks! If he's teething or under the weather, he may need comforting in the night, and fail to settle for naps unless he is being held. The most important thing you can do is to go with the flow. Try not to become anxious, which will only distress your baby and encourage him to develop negative associations with sleep. Fortunately, most sleep problems are short-term, and can be dealt with by employing a few tried-and-tested tricks (see pp.120–123).

Blissful sleep As your baby grows and develops and becomes increasingly secure in the knowledge of your love and constant care, she'll be happy to settle herself to sleep, knowing that you are always there to attend to her needs.

Your baby's bed

When deciding which type of bed to buy for your baby, think about factors such as where your baby will be sleeping for the first few months, and whether you want to opt for a bed that she can grow into, or if you'd prefer her to sleep in something smaller and cosier at first.

What to consider

Follow the guidelines below when choosing your baby's bed.

★ Ideally, your baby's cot or Moses basket should have a new mattress, even if the cot or basket are second-hand, as an old mattress can harbour bacteria and mould.

★ Check that the cot and mattress conform to government safety standards, BSEN716.

★ Avoid mattresses that contain the fire-retardant substances known as polybrominated diphenyl ethers (PBDEs).

★ Ensure the mattress fits the cot snugly so that no part of your baby's body, not even her fingers, can become trapped between the mattress and the cot.

★ Make sure all screws and bolts are secure, so that there is no danger of the cot collapsing, and she won't be scratched if she rolls near to them.

TOP TIP
If you need to use a second-hand cot, strip and repaint it in case the paint contained lead. Ensure that it conforms to current safety standards, with bars no less that 2.5cm (1in) and no more than 5cm (2in) apart.

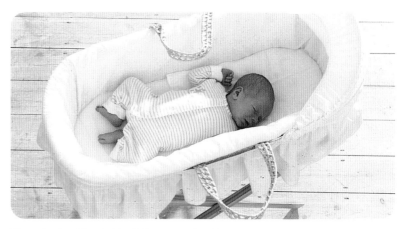

Moses basket Many babies feel more comfortable in a smaller, cosier bed, such as a Moses basket. They've been living in a confined space for the last nine months and may naturally feel more secure in a similar environment. Choose a sturdy basket, and avoid lifting it when she is in it to prevent straining your back.

Cribs If a full-sized cot seems overwhelming at first, you could try a smaller crib. Ones that rock can be soothing. Once your baby can sit up, she should be moved to a full-sized cot.

Travel cots These are ideal if you need to settle your baby away from home. Look for one with different levels, so that the mattress can be raised in the early days to save you having to bend over to settle her.

Full-sized cot There's no reason why your baby can't go straight into a full-sized cot, although she may seem a little lost in it. If you wish, you can use a cot separator, which keeps her firmly at one end of her cot. Always place her with her feet to the foot of the cot (see p.108), and layer thinner blankets rather than using a quilt or anything too heavy.

Choosing the right cot

There is a wide variety of beds and bedding available for babies. As well as thinking about style and colour schemes, when choosing your baby's bed bear in mind a few key points. Most importantly, safety, comfort and practicality should guide your decision.

Sleeping side by side If you are planning to have your baby in your room for the first six months, as is advised to help prevent cot death, you may prefer a cot that's at bed height, with a side that pulls down or stays open to fit against the side of your bed.

Height adjustable base Cots where you can adjust the height as your baby grows ensure that you can continue to use it until your baby is ready to move to a bed, at around two years.

Drop-sides These allow lifting access without straining your back.

Teething rails These help prevent damage to the cot if your baby chews on it, and prevent her splintering her mouth.

Wheels or castors An easily moveable cot is useful when you want to clean under it, or move it around the room. Before buying one, ensure that the castors are lockable to prevent the cot moving around when your baby starts to stand up and bounce.

Cot frames Ones with a non-toxic finish, such as beeswax, are ideal.

Bedding and equipment

When choosing your baby's bedding, as well as considering the colour scheme, it's important to ensure that your baby will be both safe and comfortable. This, in turn, helps you to feel relaxed while he sleeps.

Getting organized

You may find that your baby's bedding needs changing fairly frequently as a result of nappy leakages in the night. Being well equipped and organised helps to minimize sleep disruption and ensure his comfort.

★ Keep spare linen and bedclothes underneath or near the cot so that you can change wet sheets quickly at night – and keep a laundry basket close by.

★ Buy a minimum of starter bed linen for Moses baskets and smaller cribs or cots, as your baby will need a full-sized cot soon enough.

★ Adjust your baby's bedding according to the temperature and remember it's important that he doesn't overheat.

Fitted sheets These are essential, especially if your baby is a wriggler. If you tuck flat sheets under the cot, he may drag them loose when he tosses and turns, and become tangled in his bedding. You'll need at least three sheets – one on the bed, one in the wash and one for emergencies!

Cotton sheets and blankets Choose light, comfortable and, preferably, cotton bedding, which "breathes" and can be washed easily. Duvets aren't suitable for babies under one year as they are too heavy and pose a risk of suffocation. Instead, layer sheets and light blankets to keep him at the right temperature.

TOP TIP
Add or remove sheets or lightweight blankets as required to keep your baby at a comfortable temperature. Bear in mind that a folded blanket counts as two layers.

Baby sleeping bags These are good for slightly older babies who may kick off their covers. Choose a quilted cotton bag that fastens easily at the shoulders. Buy one appropriate for your baby's age and size, with a weight that suits the bedroom temperature. Bags come in "togs", much like duvets.

A baby monitor This is an important piece of equipment if your baby is in a room where he may not be heard. It's reassuring for you and you may find it easier to relax if you know that you will hear your baby. But don't leap at every noise – babies often complain a bit before settling themselves back to sleep.

Where your baby sleeps

Some parents wish to settle their baby in her own room early on, while others prefer to have her close by for the first months, as is advised to help prevent cot death. Choose an option that works for you as a family.

Close by Place your baby's basket or cot near to your bed, and at a height that makes it easy to lift her in and out. If she is a noisy sleeper, try not to attend to her the moment she snuffles: she'll need to learn to settle herself and will often do so naturally.

Sharing a space Babies often enjoy the comfort of sharing a sleeping space with you. A cot that sits beside your bed allows you instant access to your baby. If she's in your bed, a baby nest or bed divider, can help to prevent you squashing her.

The pros and cons of co-sleeping

Many parents choose to sleep with their babies, often because it gives easy access for feeding, which means less disruption. However, if you do co-sleep, follow the safety guidelines. Co-sleeping isn't advised if your baby was premature or of a low birthweight (less than 2.5kg/5.5lb).

Co-sleeping pros If you choose to have your baby in your bed in the early months, this means that you can breastfeed her on demand and comfort her without leaving your bed. Some believe that mums and babies get more sleep when in the same bed. Sleeping together may also help a strong bond to develop.

What are the cons? There are concerns that you could roll onto your baby while asleep, so take safety precautions (see right). Some experts believe that co-sleeping discourages independence and that your baby will find it hard to settle herself and sleep on her own. You also need to consider the loss of intimacy between you and your partner and the repercussions this has.

Making it safe If you do choose to co-sleep, it's crucial that you follow the guidelines to help prevent cot death, or SIDS (see p.109). Don't allow your baby to get too hot in your bed. Make sure she lies on only the sheet covered mattress, not on or under the duvet, and that there are no pillows close by her as these pose a suffocation risk.

The best sleeping positions

Settling your baby to sleep in a comfortable, safe position is paramount to his health and ability to sleep soundly. Although it may not seem as though your baby is comfortable on his back, this is the safest position.

What you can do

As well as putting your baby down on his back to sleep, ensuring that his bedding is correctly in place will help to ensure he remains comfortable and safe.

★ Tuck in blankets and sheets securely. This can help to stop your baby wriggling in the night, and also helps to prevent bedding working loose and covering your baby.

★ Don't use cot bumpers as these can make your baby's head too hot if he nestles next to them.

KEY FACT
There is no evidence that breathing or movement monitors help prevent cot death, and they should only be used on the guidance of a doctor.

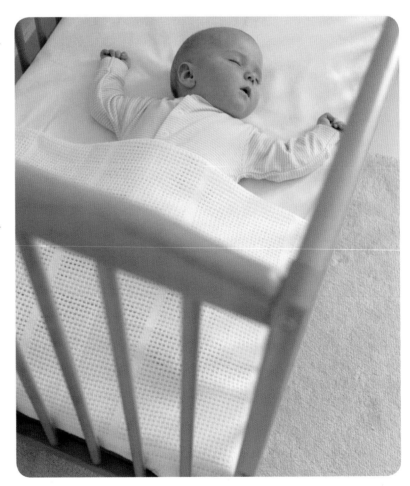

Feet to foot When you put your baby down to sleep, place him with his feet at the foot of his cot. This stops him wriggling down under his covers, which could cause overheating and/or suffocation.

Top of the cot As older babies are stronger and their motor skills are better developed, babies over one year old can be put at the top of the cot, or may work their way up. Use layers of light blankets, or an appropriate weight sleeping bag to keep him warm.

Turning over Babies over one year old will move around more. The advice is still to put your baby to sleep on his back, but if he moves around in the night and ends up on his side, try not to worry as he is now able to move blankets away or adjust his position to avoid suffocation.

Sudden Infant Death Syndrome (SIDS)

SIDS, or cot death, still isn't fully understood. It occurs most in babies under four months old. Low birthweight and premature babies and boys are most at risk. Research into SIDS has indicated a series of risk factors. By following the guidelines below, you can help to reduce the risk of SIDS.

Lie your baby on his back to sleep Put him on his back with his feet to the foot of the cot, and have him sleep in your room for the first six months, so you're aware of any discomfort he's in.

Avoid smoking Don't smoke in pregnancy (mum and dad) and don't let anyone smoke in the same room as your baby, or in the home. Never co-sleep with your baby if you or your partner smokes.

Avoid co-sleeping Don't share a bed with your baby if he was premature (or less than 2.5kg/5.5lb at birth); you've

been drinking alcohol or taking medication; or you're very tired. If you want to share a bed without the risks, consider investing in a "bedside bed" or co-sleeper, which adjusts to the height of your bed and fastens to it so there is no gap between your mattress and the baby's.

Don't let your baby get too hot (see p.111). Feel his tummy or the back of his neck – if these are hot or he's sweating, take off a layer of bedding. It's normal for babies to have cool hands and feet. Also, your baby's room doesn't need to be hot. Keep the temperature at about 18°C (64.4°F).

Bedding Don't let your baby sleep with a pillow or a duvet, and tuck in bedding securely so that it can't cover his head.

Breastfeeding Research shows that breastfed babies are less likely to die from SIDS than babies who have only ever received formula milk.

Offering a dummy Research indicates that the sucking action can help to prevent SIDS.

Getting help If your baby is unwell, seek medical advice promptly.

Making your baby comfortable

Ensuring that your baby doesn't get too hot while asleep is crucial as her temperature regulating mechanism isn't well developed and she can easily overheat. Take a few steps to keep her comfortable and content.

What you need to know

Keeping your baby at the right temperature is an important factor in safe sleeping.

★ Keep the temperature in your baby's room at around 18°C (64.4°F).

★ Use layers of thin cotton blankets or sheets, which will allow the release of heat, but still keep your baby warm.

★ Don't let your baby sleep next to a heater or a fire, or in direct sunlight.

★ Never use an electric blanket or hot water bottle in your baby's bed.

★ Don't use duvets or sheepskins before your baby is at least one year old.

Avoid overheating Like adults, babies can be uncomfortable if too hot. A single sheet is adequate when the weather is warm, or perhaps no sheet at all. Check her tummy or the back of her neck. If these are too warm to the touch, remove a layer of bedding.

Cooling down In the warmer months, you may wish to use a fan in your baby's room to cool it down before bedtime. Don't keep the fan on when your baby is in the room as she may find the draught uncomfortable and chilly in the night.

The right temperature Babies don't respond well to a hot bedroom. It's better to keep her room on the cool side, and add blankets if needed. Ideally, her room should be around 18°C (64.4°F).

A cosy buggy Your baby's temperature can drop quickly in cold weather, so ensure she is warmly dressed when outside. Bring layers of light blankets to keep her warm and make sure she wears a hat outdoors.

TOP TIP

Avoid swaddling. Although this is thought to reduce the chances of young babies waking themselves, it can increase the risk of overheating.

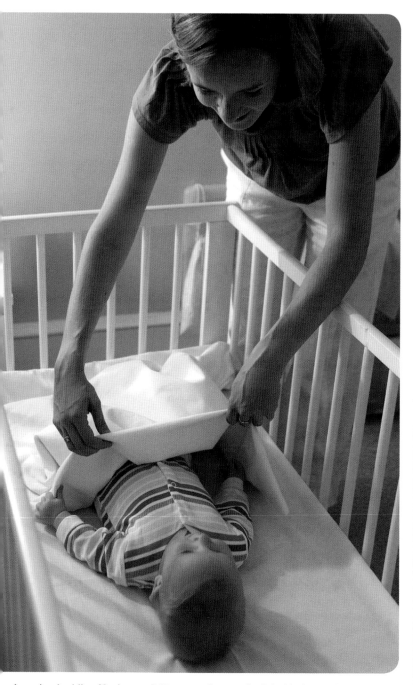

Adapting to the seasons

Use your common sense when dressing your baby for bed and deciding what bedding she needs.

In the colder months When it's chilly, dressing your baby in a vest and sleepsuit for bed is fine, with blankets or a sleeping bag added as needed. You may instinctively want to add layers, and maybe even a hat for good measure. However, your baby can become overheated with too many layers, and she shouldn't wear a hat indoors.

You may wish to choose a sleeping bag with a tog rating of 2.5, which will keep her at roughly the right temperature all year round. You can also add layers of thin blankets if needed, testing her tummy or the back of her neck regularly to ensure that she is warm, but not too hot.

Some parents crank up the heat in their baby's room during the winter to ensure that it's toasty. This is not only unnecessary, but may cause dangerous overheating.

When it's warm It's best to dress your baby in as little as possible in the summer months, and then add sheets or blankets if she becomes cool. You may wish to look for sleepsuits without feet, which will keep her cooler.

Lower tog sleeping bags, such as 0.5 and 1, are ideal for hotter weather and warm rooms.

Layering bedding Use layers of thin cotton sheets and cellular blankets or fleeces made from cotton – the lighter the better – that can be added and removed as required. If her tummy or the back of her neck is warm, she is warm enough.

A bedtime routine

Once your baby is feeding well and sleeps regularly, this is the perfect moment to establish a bedtime routine. Your baby will develop healthy sleep associations and settle down happily once he knows what to expect.

Benefits of a routine

Establishing a gentle routine before bedtime that involves a regular sequence of events, such as a bath, massage and story or song, helps your baby to settle at night as he will come to link these activities with a soothing night's sleep.

★ Establishing a routine in infancy, led by your baby's own inborn schedule and his individual needs, will develop healthy sleep habits in the early days, and encourage good sleep patterns as he grows and develops.

★ Babies respond well to routines as they grow to learn exactly what to expect and when. In fact, babies feel much more secure when they know their boundaries. If your baby's routine shifts repeatedly, he'll feel unsettled and will be more likely to create a pre-bedtime fuss or wake in the night.

★ Sticking to a set bedtime means that you'll know when you have some free time to get on with other things.

★ Repeating the same order of events every night means that your baby will associate bedtime with pleasurable sensations, rather than being worried about being left alone.

An evening feed A good bedtime routine separates feeding from sleep. Giving an evening feed downstairs avoids feeding becoming a sleep association. You can then continue his bedtime routine upstairs.

A bedtime bath Although your baby doesn't need a full bath every day, a warm bath or top and tail (see p.24) will soothe and relax him in preparation for sleep. He'll also use up energy splashing in the bath!

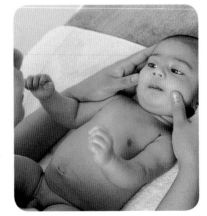

An evening massage Many parents recommend a night-time massage to relax their baby, often after a warm bath. After drying him, use a little oil to nourish his skin and gently massage his body (see p.146).

Time for pyjamas When your baby is clean and dry, get him dressed for bed. Sing a relaxing song as you dress him. He'll soon understand what's happening and enjoy the process of getting ready to settle down.

Being consistent

It's amazing how quickly babies recognize their routine, and how much more easily they settle once they begin to associate their routine with a positive bedtime experience.

A set pattern Whether your routine involves a bath, bedtime story, a back or tummy rub, a kiss (or all of these things), it's very important to do it in the same order and at the same time every night. Babies love repetition, and are creatures of routine. Your baby will be settled and reassured by consistent events, both at night-time and during the day. You may find that he knows his routine so well that he reaches out for his book after a feed!

Saying goodnight You may wish to sing to your baby, or rock him for a while before you settle him down (although if you do rock him, be aware that this will become a sleep association that he'll continue to need). Before you leave, make sure that he is comfortable in his bed, say a cheery goodnight, then leave.

TOP TIP

Forget about routines for the first few weeks. You'll need time to bond and to get to know each other; your baby's own routine will eventually start to assert itself.

Story time Looking at a bedtime book together, whether a simple cloth one or a picture story book, can be established early on. Even if your baby doesn't understand it, he'll be engaged by the pictures and soothed by your voice and closeness.

Settling your baby

The way you settle your baby from the earliest days helps to establish sleep associations. Try to use the same cues each night so that your baby familiarizes herself with the settling process. Make sure that your partner, or anyone else who settles your baby, uses the same cues, too.

How much sleep do babies need?

Although your baby needs a considerable amount of sleep, she won't sleep for particularly long stretches until around six months old.

At one month Your very young baby may sleep for an average of 15–17 hours each day. Usually, babies sleep for approximately eight and a half hours at night (though waking every two to three hours!) and for about seven hours during the day, divided into three or more naps.

From three to six months Your baby still needs about 15 hours sleep in 24 hours. She is starting to distinguish between day and night with the help of bedtime routines, and may start to sleep for slightly longer stretches at night as she can now go for longer without a feed.

After six months Your baby is capable of sleeping for 10 or 11 hours a night (though is still likely to wake), and needs two decent naps in the day each of usually 2-3 hours long to give her the quota of around 14 hours sleep that she needs.

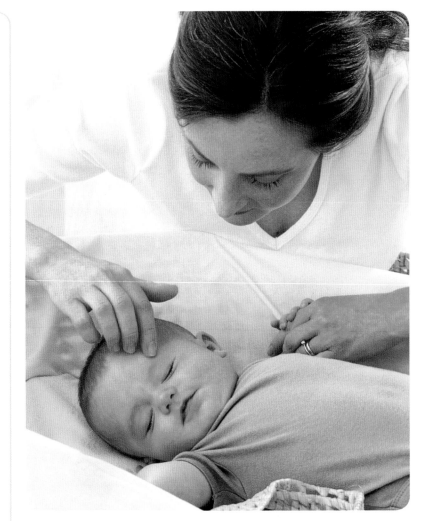

Soothing to sleep Stroking your young baby's head and holding his hand can ease the separation from you. Repeating the same song or goodnight words each night leads him to recognize these as a precursor to restful sleep.

A dim light Some babies find a nightlight reassuring. You may also find it useful to have a dim light to check on her throughout the evening, or if you need to pick her up from her cot for a feed.

A reassuring presence If your older baby wakes when she isn't due a feed, go to her room to check on her and reassure her and then leave, saying your usual goodnight phrase that she associates with settling down to sleep.

A little comfort

Sucking a hand or thumb helps soothe babies to sleep. A dummy can be an option if your baby is miserable or irritable and simply won't settle.

At six months, your baby will also be old enough to form an attachment to a blanket or toy that she can use as a comforter to help her get to sleep.

Your baby's soother Most babies associate falling asleep with the feeling of satisfaction after a feed. Often, babies enjoy stroking something soft while they feed, and this combined stroking and sucking comforts them to sleep. Soft toys, cloths or dummies provide this source of stroking and associated comfort; these "transitional" objects, link your baby to the feeding experience and so ease her separation from you to the cot. If you dislike dummies, a thumb can be a better option for your baby to suck on.

Safe sleeping Recent studies also suggest that babies who sleep with a dummy have a reduced risk of cot death, or SIDS (see p.109).

Your baby's soother A favourite blanket or a soft toy that is always present when your baby goes to sleep can help her to settle.

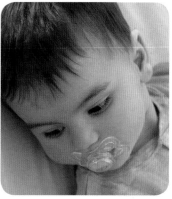

Dummies These are powerful soothers as your baby can suckle. However, they can be habit-forming.

Daytime sleep

Your baby needs both daytime and night-time sleep. Some babies find it hard to settle in the day and wake often during naps. Settling into a routine and getting him to settle down regularly will ensure that he gets the sleep he needs.

Establishing a daytime routine

After two or three months, as your baby develops, he'll begin to settle naturally into a feeding and sleeping pattern during the day.

Daytime activity When your baby wakes in the morning, open the curtains and engage in your normal activities so that he associates daytime with bustle and noise. From about six weeks to three months, he'll still alternate feeds and sleep in the day, but will begin to have more wakeful periods, so that eventually his routine may be a feed, a wakeful period, another feed and then a sleep.

Regulating feeds You can still feed on demand while working out a daytime routine. Try offering feeds at the times that work best for you, and he'll eventually feed more at these times. It's wise to allow some flexibility during the day for times when you baby is fussy or you have activities or appointments. Simply try to do things in roughly the same order, and lead up to daytime naps with the same sequence of events.

Late naps Babies over four months should avoid napping after about 3.30pm, as this can affect their ability to settle in the early evening.

Early days At first, you may want to keep your baby in the same room as you when he sleeps in the day, perhaps settling him in a comfortable bouncy chair. Sleeping in this position also helps prevent reflux (see p.83).

When you're out The gentle rhythm of a moving pram or buggy can soothe your baby to sleep, and this may account for some of his daytime naps. However, try to avoid using this as a sleep tool at other times.

A familiar place As your baby grows, it's a good idea to settle him in his cot, which he associates with sleep. Be reassuring, so he doesn't feel abandoned. Lie him down when he's had a feed, been winded and is sleepy.

Being consistent Before you leave the room, use an "exit" phrase, such as "sleep time" that you also use at night. If he's growing well and is healthy, he'll be fine being left on his own to sleep.

A darkened room Light stimulates us to wake. In the day, draw the curtains or pull down the blinds, but don't tiptoe around him; you want him to get used to household sounds and to sleep through them.

Sleeping independently

Nothing divides parents quite like the issue of sleep and whether, or how, you should encourage your baby into a routine. In practice, at around six months, you may want to take steps to help your baby sleep longer at night.

What you need to know

If your baby doesn't yet sleep any more soundly or for any longer periods at night than in the day, or has difficulty settling, you may wish to be more proactive about helping her to establish better sleep associations.

★ If your baby is feeding well, putting on weight and is otherwise well she is now capable of sleeping for longer periods at night.

★ Be reassured that most babies are irritable when tired and may cry when settling to sleep. Giving her some time alone helps her learn to settle herself.

★ Try keeping a sleep diary for a week or so to chart her feeding and sleeping times. This helps you to understand your baby's body clock and ensure that she is ready to settle in the evening. At around six months, many babies have one long sleep in the morning, then another early afternoon, finishing by mid-afternoon.

TOP TIP

Try to avoid making eye contact with your baby when you return to her room to settle her. Be calm and soothing, but don't engage her in any communication.

1 **After her feed**, hold your baby close and look at a book together. Speak quietly and gently, so that she understands it's time to unwind before bed. If you wish, you could leave the book in her cot to act as a transitional object (see p.115).

2 **Place your baby** in her cot, maybe with a last stroke of her tummy or head. Choose a song to sing each night: she'll enjoy the repetition, and begin to associate it with sleep. Have an "exit" phrase, such as "sleep time", and leave calmly.

3 **If your baby cries**, go back in and reassure her by stroking her hand but don't pick her up. Smile and look loving but don't chat. Leave again. If she cries, or is still crying, go back again.

4 **You may have to go back in** several times. Try reading to soothe her with your voice. It can take a few days for your baby to realize that you always return and she can fall asleep safely.

Encouraging your baby to go to sleep

Some parents aren't comfortable leaving their baby to cry. If this is the case, find an approach that's right for you and your family. Be aware, though, that methods that need your presence for her to fall asleep can take longer to work, and that you'll need to continue this approach in the future.

Self-soothing It's a good idea to leave the room while your baby is awake so that she learns how to settle herself to sleep when you are not there, and becomes independent of the need for your physical presence to fall asleep.

Transitional objects Some parents find comforters and dummies (see p.115) can ease separation anxieties and help babies sleep. However, sometimes dummies can themselves cause sleep problems if your baby loses her dummy during the night and has to wake you to find it for her!

Gradual withdrawal If your baby cries as soon as you leave her at night, try withdrawing slowly from her room. Sit by her bed and touch her or say "shhh" to settle her. If she cries when you try to leave, move your chair a bit nearer to the door until you can safely exit without her crying. You will need to repeat this in the night if she wakes up, and it may take a number of weeks before she feels secure enough to fall asleep happily.

Close contact You may prefer to pick your baby up when she wakes, or to always attend to her when she cries out. However, you will need to do this consistently as it will become her established sleep association.

A flexible approach Your baby's night-time routine will falter from time to time, and she may genuinely be uncomfortable or distressed and need the comfort of being held for a while. Be aware that her needs will change occasionally, and you should be ready to attend to her when this happens.

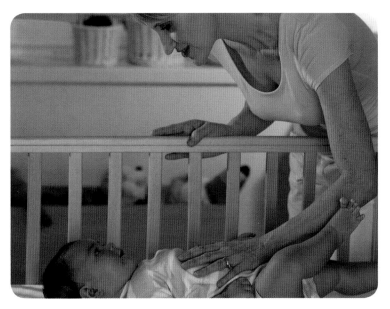

Words and touch Lean over her cot and whisper "shhhh". Sometimes, just knowing that you are there will be enough for her to fall asleep. Rubbing her tummy while you do this can be deeply soothing for your baby.

A soothing cuddle You may choose to give your baby a comforting cuddle or to rock her to sleep at night. You'll need to repeat this when she wakes during the night.

A gentle stroke Laying your hand on your baby's head, or stroking her gently for a minute or two before you leave her can reassure her and help her to settle.

Night waking

It's natural for babies to wake at night, especially early on when they need regular feeds. If, however, your baby continues to wake often for just a little milk or comfort, you may need to take action!

TOP TIP

Some babies need to suckle to get to sleep or to settle, and so feed almost constantly when upset. If he's not hungry, he may find comfort from a dummy instead.

When older babies wake

Young babies normally wake because they are hungry, uncomfortable or lonely. As your baby grows, he may wake for different reasons.

Teething Between four and seven or eight months, your baby's first teeth may start to come through. This can cause discomfort and so may disturb his sleep for a while.

More mobility Babies who have learned to roll or sit may decide to practise their new skills during the night, which can keep them awake! Also, as your baby gets more mobile, he may kick off his covers or get stuck in a new position. Putting him in a sleeping bag can help to prevent night-time activities.

Changes in routine Many babies are extremely sensitive to routine, so if things have changed in your household, or your baby has had a period of illness, he may become unsettled for a while.

Milk feeds Breastfed babies may need feeding more often at night, but once he is over six months and growing well, he is capable of sleeping for up to eight hours. Discourage frequent waking by giving a good feed before bed, and when he wakes.

Quiet activity Turn down the lights, avoid eye contact and speak quietly to your baby when you change him at night. He needs to learn that it isn't playtime, and that his needs will be quietly addressed before he is settled back down.

Back to bed Once your baby has been fed, winded, and, if necessary, changed, settle him down in the usual way. He may object for a while, but reassure him in soothing tones. Avoid carrying him for long during the night unless he is very upset.

Keeping her close Having your baby with you in your bedroom means that you can see to her with minimal disruption, and check on her without leaving your bed. She will also be reassured by your presence and rhythmic breathing, and settle more easily.

Taking turns If your baby is unwell, take turns settling him when he wakes. It doesn't take both parents to soothe a fractious baby, and you both need to get as much sleep as you possibly can, especially when your baby is unwell.

Active days, quiet nights

The more alert and active your baby is during the day, the more likely he is to sleep soundly at night.

Playtime It may be many months before your baby is truly mobile, but stimulating him during the day, and encouraging him to be active with games, age-appropriate toys and simple physical play can mean that he is physically tired at night-time and will fall asleep more easily – and, most importantly, stay asleep!

A dose of fresh air Many parents firmly believe that a trip outdoors at least once a day helps their baby to sleep more soundly at night.

Timing naps If your baby wakes often at night or rises early, check the timing of his daytime naps and consider whether he is napping too close to bedtime.

Growing and learning It is important to stimulate your baby but watch for signs that he's had enough – you don't want to overtire him.

Early rising

Some babies get out of kilter and have their longest sleeps during the day, and wake early in the morning! Moving feeding and sleeping times and avoiding late afternoon naps can reset your baby's body clock.

Set a rota Dealing with a baby who is fully awake at half past five each morning can be exhausting over time. Until her sleep pattern resolves itself, take it in turns with your partner to get up and attend to her.

Shut out the light Your baby will naturally stir when the light becomes brighter. Fitting a black-out curtain or blind in the room stops the sunlight waking her as soon as the sun comes up in the morning.

A morning activity Some older babies are happy to entertain themselves when they wake. Firmly attach an activity board to the inside end of her cot, or some appropriate toys where she won't see them in the night.

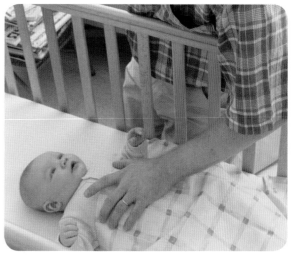

Shorter naps As your baby gets older, he requires less sleep. If he regularly wakes very early in the morning try shortening his nap times, especially if he is in the habit of sleeping later in the day. Late afternoon sleeps are associated with difficulties settling in the evenings and disrupted night-time sleep.

Go with the flow Unfortunately, if all other methods have failed, it may simply be the case that your baby has had enough sleep and is ready to start the day bright and early. You can try settling him back down once or twice in the morning, but if he refuses to settle, you may have to accept this and start your day early too!

Bonding with your baby

YOUR NEW FAMILY

Spending time with your baby – getting to know him, understanding what makes him happy and ensuring that he is safe, contented and well-fed – is the single most important thing you can do to establish a healthy bond between you.

Bonding is the intense positive attachment that develops between parents and their babies. It encourages you to love your baby, feel affection, and protect, nourish and nurture him. In fact, it's this attachment that gets you up in the middle of the night to feed your baby, and that drives you to spend limitless time trying to comfort him when he is distressed.

In return, babies who experience this intense attachment with their parents develop a deep sense of security and positive self-esteem that remain with them for the rest of their lives.

A BRAND NEW RELATIONSHIP
The relationship that evolves between you and your baby will grow and develop as your baby gets older. Bonding is a process, rather than a single event, and you may not even know it is happening until you experience an overwhelming sense of love for your baby – prompted, perhaps, by his first smile or by his little hand reaching up to touch your face.

The first few days and weeks of your baby's life are, however, undoubtedly important for bonding. This is when the process of bonding kick-starts, which helps you to cope better when you're feeling overwhelmed by your new responsibilities. New parenthood is exhausting, no matter how much your baby sleeps or how little he cries. Not only do you have to learn a whole new set of skills – many of which need to take place in the middle of the night – but you have responsibility for a completely helpless baby who needs you for his survival. Combine this with the tiredness that can accompany feeding, interrupted sleep and the natural anxiety as to whether your baby is happy and well and that you are doing things right, and it can be a very daunting prospect. Establishing bonding early on can make all of these things easier.

YOUR CHANGING ROLES
There is no doubt that your relationship with your partner will be altered by the arrival of your baby. Your team of two suddenly becomes three (or more), and your roles as lovers, friends and partners therefore need to be re-established. You both now have extra responsibilities and, in addition, your patience will be tested by sleepless nights and a marked change in the focus of your attention.

Although you may both dote on your baby, it's still possible, and normal, to harbour some resentment that you are no longer the most important person in each other's lives. Furthermore, you may find that the activities that bonded you as a couple have to be put to one side for some time. All in all, it can be a testing time for even the strongest of relationships.

There are many things that you can do to ensure that your relationship remains strong and mutually nurturing, and these are every bit as important as the care you give to your baby, as they build the foundation for a positive family life for him. We'll look at these later on in this chapter, but it's worth noting that building a strong relationship with your partner, and taking steps to work together to adjust to the role of parenting, will reap huge benefits in the long term – for you both and for your baby.

Skin-to-skin Close contact is proven to encourage the process of bonding, both for you and your baby. If your new arrival hasn't been placed directly on your chest after birth, remove his vest and sleepsuit and try your first breastfeed "in the nude".

All together Involve dad as much as possible as he may be feeling a little left out. You carried your baby for nine months and he will depend most on you for nourishment and comfort in the early days, but dads play an important role too.

GETTING CLOSE

Establishing a strong, loving bond with your baby will help to keep him content and settled; what's more, it will make the job of parenting him that much easier. There are a multitude of ways that bonding can and will occur, from that first breastfeed through to playful games, massage and even simply holding him close.

In this chapter we'll look at the very best ways to help develop a strong relationship with your baby. We will also help you through periods where things seem insurmountably difficult. Some women (and men) take longer to feel an intense attachment to their baby, but that doesn't mean that it won't happen. Life has a habit of throwing the unexpected at us when we least expect it. In the meantime, learning to work your way through difficult times with a host of tried-and-tested methods can help to make the process of bonding that much easier. The manner in which you respond to your baby is the cornerstone for bonding; recognising and learning to meet his needs helps him to feel secure that you are always there, and in turn develops a bond of love.

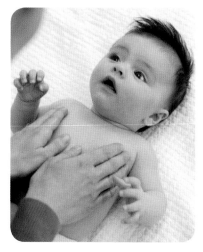

Soothing strokes Gentle baby massage will help soothe your baby, and studies have shown that it helps to promote the process of bonding. Try to make massage and stroking a regular part of your baby's routine.

Relish the closeness The most important thing you can do to encourage bonding is to enjoy your baby – soak in his warmth and unconditional love for you. Place his skin next to yours so that you both feel the intensity of your new relationship.

Bonding with your newborn baby

Bonding may not happen immediately, nor does it have to occur in a certain space of time. However, it's clear that the period straight after the birth is a time when you're primed to develop a close relationship.

Encouraging bonding

Although it's a natural process, there are ways to help establish bonding.

★ **Pace yourself.** Take each day as it comes; don't fret about chores, just concentrate on being with your baby.

★ **Breastfeed.** The skin-to-skin contact and closeness creates the ideal conditions for bonding.

★ **Hold her close** so she feels secure and enjoys eye-to-eye contact.

★ **Stroke her.** Touch is an important means of communication for newborns.

★ **Talk to your baby.** She will be familiar with your voice from her time in the womb, so she'll feel comforted when you sing or talk to her.

★ **Spend time with your baby.** Every moment builds the foundation for successful bonding.

Close together Skin-to-skin contact promotes bonding. Breastfeeding also encourages this process as you do it so regularly, so it guarantees close physical contact over every 24-hour period.

Dads too Father–baby bonding is equally important to your baby's wellbeing, and to your partner's relationship with his baby. Enjoying a regular activity, such as bathing or a pre-bed cuddle, helps cement this bond.

TOP TIP
Being emotional and tired can affect bonding. Resting, eating healthily and getting gentle exercise help you feel at your best and able to enjoy the time with your baby.

Mutually adoring Enjoy plenty of eye-to-eye contact with your newborn baby, which not only establishes meaningful communication with her, but helps you to get to know her too. Hold her 20–30 cm (8–10 in) away – the distance she can focus at first.

The family dynamic Continuing to build your relationship with your partner will help to make the family dynamic positive and loving. Although there is a temptation for new mums to take on the lion's share of the work, the most successful partnerships work as a team and take pleasure in bonding with their baby together.

Giving it time

If you don't feel a bond at first sight, don't worry. For some, this deep attachment develops more slowly.

Obstacles to bonding Parent-baby bonding is a complicated process and different for every individual. Factors that can affect the process and the speed at which it takes place include having an emergency Caesarean or a difficult birth, being separated from your baby at birth, tiredness, anxiety and feeling overwhelmed by the responsibilities of parenthood.

Helping yourself It helps to ensure that you get plenty of sleep, which will take the edge off any anxiety you may be feeling, and help you to feel calmer about new parenthood. Don't try to be "super-woman": be realistic about what you can achieve and don't feel guilty if jobs don't get done. Enjoy spending time with your baby and simply relish your moments together. Limit visitors, unless they can offer you a helping hand, and keep your baby close.

Get support If you are feeling overwhelmed, talk to family and friends and ask them to step in and help if you need a break.

Be realistic Most importantly, try to remember that bonding can take some time, and it doesn't make you a bad parent if you don't feel an instant attachment to your baby. Some of the slowest bonders can establish the very strongest relationships with their babies, and feel that intense love and attachment when the time is right.

Adjusting to parenthood

Becoming new parents is a dramatic step in your relationship. While the wonder of creating a new life brings you close, the reality of caring for a new baby can put even the strongest relationships under pressure.

Your new roles

Parenthood comes with responsibilities that will define your lives for years to come. Embracing these changes, rather than worrying that life will never be the same again, will make the process much easier.

Mutual understanding Talk regularly to establish how both of you are feeling. If you find it too much to keep your baby fed and content and the home clean, let your partner know how you feel and discuss together how to support each other.

Try to be patient. You may both be feeling fractious through lack of sleep and, perhaps, even anxious about your new roles. Sharing your concerns, and understanding that the irritability will be short-lived when things settle down can make all the difference.

Share the care Try not to establish a "mum as sole carer" scenario. Although you will be responsible for the majority of your baby's care simply through being the source of his milk, he does need to bond with dad as well, and he with him.

Proud parents There is no doubt that you will enjoy showing off your new baby. Presenting your precious bundle to the world is a wonderful way to celebrate your baby's birth – and your new role as a mother.

Working together Try to share the babycare and household chores. You're a team, and both of you need time to relax. Caring for your baby is time-consuming work, so it helps to keep the household ticking over by sharing the load.

Grown-up time When your baby is asleep, try to spend time together talking instead of heading off to bed immediately! Even if you're exhausted, celebrate your new parenthood: listen to each other and make sure that you're both coping.

All together Although it can be tempting to rest when your partner has the baby, part of the bonding process involves your baby getting to know mum and dad as a safe, secure unit. Take pride in your new baby, and enjoy his company together. After all, that's where the fun of parenting begins!

Coping as a single mum

Being a single mum means coping and making decisions alone. However, you'll spend lots of time with your baby, and experience an intense, wonderful relationship. There are ways to make life easier.

Get enough rest Sleep when your baby sleeps, and don't hesitate to let household standards slip a little. It won't be long before a routine of some description is established and you can then factor in your other responsibilities.

Accept help Take any support you can and enjoy some time to yourself. Don't hesitate to call on friends and family. Even a few hours' rest, while someone else does the soothing can make you feel much more alert and confident. If someone offers to make some meals, don't be shy to take them up on the offer!

Involve dad If your baby's dad is still in the picture, you might want to encourage him to spend some time with your baby. Although you may not have a relationship, he may always have one with your baby.

Build up a network When you feel ready, meet up with other single mums. There is nothing like a mum's network for getting some great advice, and sharing your concerns and problems can be a huge weight off your mind.

A supportive network

Even if your baby is a great sleeper, there is nothing more exhausting than new parenthood. There is – and should be – no shame in getting support when you need it and learning to share the load a little.

Coping during the early weeks

The following tips can help you cope in the first few tiring weeks.

★ Set up a visitor's rota, so you're not inundated with guests needing tea.

★ Make sure you have the numbers for your local breastfeeding counsellor, your health visitor and/or your doctor, so that you can ask for advice if you need it.

★ Welcome all offers of meals and, if there's time before the birth, prepare and freeze as many meals as you can.

★ Consider putting a list on the fridge, in bold letters, saying something like: 'If you'd like to help ...' and listing the things that would be useful! Most of your guests would probably love to help, but aren't sure where to start!

★ Arrange to have a few friends or eager grandparents on standby to step in when you feel that you need a break.

TOP TIP
Sleep when your baby sleeps. Even if your ironing pile has reached mammoth heights and the fridge is empty, you'll feel calmer and more capable if you rest.

Keep talking Spend time with your partner, talking through how you are feeling. Keeping a dialogue going in this way can help you to work out how you can both get the support and love you need from each other.

Helping hands Grandparents will love the chance to bond with their grandchild and are often keen to help. It can be tempting to keep an insular unit, but extra help is invaluable.

Hands-on help When at home, dads can make a significant contribution to everyday babycare. In turn, he spends rewarding time with his baby and enhances their bond.

Kind offers If friends ask to help, suggest they come round for a few hours, in the afternoon perhaps, to help get a meal on the table, address your ironing pile or hold your baby while you get some much needed rest.

Mums together Meet up with other new mums regularly to share experiences and swap advice. Simply talking to other parents in the same position can be enormously reassuring, and also gives you a bit of a break from your usual routine.

Postnatal depression

Postnatal depression (PND) affects at least 10 to 15 per cent of all new mums. Being aware of the symptoms means that you can seek advice promptly.

Early emotions It's normal to experience some of the symptoms of PND after the birth, before your hormones settle down and you get to grips with life with a new baby. Feeling weepy in the couple of weeks after the birth is known as the "baby blues". However, if symptoms persist beyond this time, you should talk to your doctor and your partner about the possibility of PND.

Symptoms of PND These include lethargy; tearfulness; anxiety; guilt; irritability; confusion; disturbed sleep; excessive exhaustion; difficulty making decisions; loss of self-esteem; lack of confidence in your ability as a mother; fear of harming yourself or your baby; loss of appetite; hostility or indifference to people you usually love; difficulty concentrating; shame at being unable to be happy; and profound helplessness.

Getting better There are many helpful treatments for PND, including antidepressants. In many cases, just understanding that you're suffering from a short-term illness can make you feel a bit better. Try to take time for yourself and relax, and accept offers of help or support. Talking to your partner, doctor or an understanding friend about how you're feeling can often be the first step to recovery.

Enjoying family life

Changing your lifestyle to accommodate your new arrival can be an exciting and challenging prospect. The secret is to take it slowly and embrace every new development positively. You'll soon find that life as a family is every bit as wonderful as you thought it would be.

Supporting siblings

Your other children will enjoy having a new brother or sister, but it is important to balance things so that they don't feel that their position has been usurped.

★ **Prepare young children several weeks in advance.** Explain that the new baby will need a lot of attention, and probably won't be much fun for a few months.

★ **Ask your little one to choose a gift for the new baby,** and find something your child really wants as a gift from the baby.

★ **Allow little ones to bathe together.** You may have a little clearing up to do, but they will enjoy the experience.

★ **Cuddle your new baby and older child together,** so that they feel a part of the same unit; your new baby will soon associate his siblings with comfort.

Involve older children Letting older siblings help in small ways with the personal care of your new baby can warm even the most stubborn sibling heart.

Deepening your bond Your baby is your first priority and every single moment you spend with her will strengthen your bond. Put aside the other commitments in your life for the time being, and just enjoy being a mum.

Family outings Having fun together and enjoying family activities is good for the whole family, and reassures older siblings that life continues as normal.

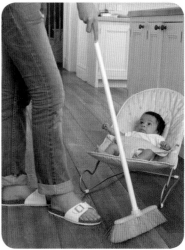

Everyday life Babies are very adaptable, and enjoy being with you whatever you're doing. It's fine sometimes simply to keep him close while you get on with jobs around the house. He'll enjoy the new experience.

Adjusting to life with twins

Having more than one newborn baby in the house most definitely presents a challenge, and at times may try your patience. However, most parents of twins find that things settle down with time, and you'll soon establish a routine and a plan for keeping everything up and running. Twins may be double the work, but there will also be double the love and fun.

Get extra help Try to get some additional help for the first few weeks. Stop worrying about the state of your house. Accepting that two babies represent a full-time job can make adapting that much easier.

Set up a routine Try to establish some sort of routine early on, and base this around periods when you know that you'll have some help.

Synchronize sleep Put your babies down together to sleep. Synchronising sleep gives you a much needed break. Do accept, though, that in the early weeks they may not follow this pattern.

"Two-at-once" Whenever you can, attend to babycare tasks for both babies together. You'll need help to get two babies bathed, fed and changed for bedtime, but this can be easier than stretching the proceedings into the evening.

Get organized Set out sleepsuits and towels in advance, top up your changing table and bag every day, and throw in a load of laundry when you get a second.

Comfort simultaneously Practise comforting your babies together as this can make you feel more in control. At the outset, it can be hard to cuddle two babies at the same time, but you'll soon find a way.

An extra challenge Caring for twins takes organization and plenty of teamwork.

Understanding your baby's cries

In the early weeks, you may be distraught to find your baby inconsolable and feel unsure what to do. The good news is that as you get to know your baby, you'll learn to recognize her cries and know just how to soothe her.

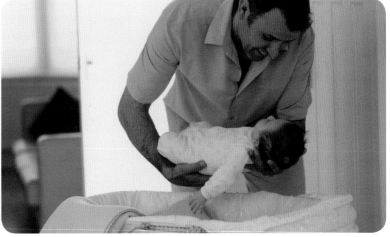

A soothing cuddle Don't underestimate the importance of comfort. Your baby may simply be lonely, and need a little company. It isn't spoiling a baby to meet her needs.

A quick response There's no point leaving a new baby to cry. She communicates with you through her cries, and will feel insecure if you don't respond.

Feeling uncomfortable One of the first things to do when you baby cries is to check her nappy. Both urine and poo can irritate her tender skin, and cause discomfort.

Time for a feed Hungry babies almost always cry as this is their only real form of communication. If her nappy is clean and dry and she's still crying, she's probably hungry.

Your unwell baby If she won't settle and her behaviour and feeding have been off kilter, check if she is warm and take her temperature (see p.49) in case she has a fever.

When to be concerned

All babies cry at some stage, and it doesn't mean they're demanding. In most cases, a little comfort, being winded or changed will soothe her. It's good to be aware, though, of when cries might indicate something more serious.

Excessive or unusual crying If your baby is fed and comfortable, but is still crying, you might worry that she's ill or in pain. All babies cry excessively sometimes, but if your baby's crying sounds unusual, such as more high-pitched or urgent than normal, and/or is accompanied by other symptoms, such as a fever (see p.50), then consult your doctor. Similarly, call the doctor if your baby's crying is accompanied by a rash; ear pulling (which can indicate an ear infection); feeding problems; fewer wet or dirty nappies than usual; or other concerns about her general health.

Lack of crying If your baby normally cries quite frequently and is uncharacteristically quiet, this could be a sign that she is unwell. Trust your instincts and if you have any concerns at all, contact your doctor, midwife or health visitor for advice.

Keep calm It's important to stay calm when your baby is distressed, as she's likely to sense your anxiety and feel even more unsettled. You may find it helpful to talk to your partner, or a family member or friend for support.

Assess her calmly There are a number of reasons why your baby may be crying. Staying calm while you work out what she needs will reassure her and help to prevent her becoming even more distressed by your anxiety.

Soothing your young baby

It can be distressing when your baby cries, but try to remember that this is the only way that he can communicate with you. There are lots of tried-and-tested ways to soothe your baby, once you've worked out what he needs.

Close contact Your baby enjoys being close to you and may cry because he wants your company. A sling helps you to get on with your day while holding him against your chest. If you're breastfeeding, he'll also smell your milk, which will reassure him.

TOP TIP

If, after switching to or changing formula, your baby starts crying after feeding, talk to your health visitor or midwife to assess if he has the right formula.

Rhythmic movement Gentle rocking may settle your baby when he's crying. He's been used to regular movement in the womb and will be comforted by its familiarity. Try singing a lullaby to your baby while you rock him in his chair.

A soothing voice Chat to your baby, sing and smile at him. If he senses that you're anxious about his cries, he'll respond in kind. Reassure him that you're there, and will always come when he needs you. Sometimes babies just want a little company.

Feeling secure Some babies find it alarming to sleep alone in the early days, so let her drift off in your arms when he is distressed. It's worth noting, too, that some babies cry because they are overstimulated, and may simply need a quiet space to rest.

Feeling hungry Crying may be a sign that your baby is hungry, or simply wants the comfort of a feed, being held close in your arms. While it isn't a good idea to get into the habit of using milk to comfort him, in the early days that may be just what he needs.

Walking around Hold your baby and walk with him. He's been close to you for nine months and may miss the gentle movement and closeness. Holding him upright and gently patting his back may also release any trapped wind that is causing discomfort.

What your baby needs

As your baby becomes more settled, his crying will change and you will be able to distinguish between the cries that indicate his different needs.

Identifying your baby's needs

There are many reasons why babies cry. Your baby may be hungry, or have a wet or dirty nappy. Babies can also cry if they have a nappy rash, are suffering from colic or are feeling unwell. Or he may simply be lonely, and want to be held. The most important thing that your baby needs is reassurance that you are there when he needs you, and that you will keep him content and comfortable by meeting his needs.

Comforting your baby Many babies respond to being held and rocked, although you may find that what worked one day may not work the next. Rhythmical sounds, such as low music or even the sound of the vacuum cleaner, can be soothing. Some babies seem to need to suck to get to sleep, or to settle, which is why they feed almost constantly when upset. If he's not hungry, he may find comfort from a dummy, or sucking on his fingers.

Try to find the techniques that work best for you and, above all, stay calm, and be reassured that you will become more confident over time.

Dealing with colic

It is not unusual for young babies to suffer from colic, characterized by unending crying, usually at the same time each day. The good news is that it does pass and there are plenty of ways to soothe your baby.

Signs of colic

If your baby has any of the following, she may be suffering with colic. If you're concerned, talk to your doctor.

★ **Inconsolable crying** that lasts for up to three hours, at least three days a week, and which is often at a similar time every day or night.

★ **Your baby's knees** may be drawn up to her chest and her fists clenched.

★ **Your baby may appear** to be in severe pain with a tummy ache.

★ **Refusing** to feed.

★ A red face.

★ Difficulty falling and staying asleep.

★ Passing wind.

Call your doctor if:

★ **Your baby's crying** or behaviour changes from its normal pattern.

★ **If the signs of colic** are accompanied by fever, diarhhoea or vomiting, blood in the stools or insufficient weight gain.

KEY FACT

About a fifth of babies suffer from colic, and it affects boys and girls equally. It usually appears at two to four weeks, and may last for three months or longer.

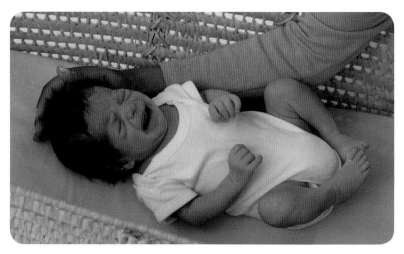

Respond to her cries If your baby's legs are drawn up and she is distressed, this is a classic sign of colic. Soothe her and pick her up when she's crying, as most colicky babies feel better when they are held and comforted.

Take a break Colic can be exhausting for babies and parents. If you're struggling to cope, put her down in her cot for a few minutes. If you use a dummy, let her have it to soothe her, then take a short break.

Releasing wind Hold your baby upright and gently pat or rub his back. If trapped wind is at the root of the problem, this may help to release it. He may also be soothed by being walked around the room.

A warm bath Warm water can act as a gentle relaxant, helping to ease the spasms of colic and calm a distressed baby. You could try getting into the bath with her to keep her calm.

Soothing massage Give your baby a gentle massage of the abdominal area, using a little oil. A good time to massage her may be before the evening feed if she is feeling relaxed and calm.

Set up a rota Take turns comforting your baby; it can be distressing to see her uncomfortable and upset, but it doesn't take both of you to soothe her. As long as your baby is being comforted, one of you can take a much-needed break.

What causes colic?

The causes of colic are still unknown and may vary from baby to baby.

Sensitivity There's some indication that colic is caused by a combination of a baby's temperament and an immature nervous system. If your baby is highly sensitive to her environment, she may react to normal stimulation or changes to the environment by crying.

Discomfort Trapped wind is often thought to be a factor. Pause to wind your baby at least twice during each feed, and try to stop her guzzling. Check the size of the hole in her teat. If it's too small, she may be swallowing air, so change to a larger size. Or you could try anti-colic bottles, designed to reduce the intake of air.

Dairy intolerance It's thought that some babies are intolerant on a short-term basis to proteins in dairy products. If you're breastfeeding, you could exclude dairy products from your diet to see if this makes a difference. If you wish to continue excluding dairy, talk to your doctor about ensuring a sufficient intake of calcium in your diet. Bottle-feeding mums might consider changing to a hypoallergenic formula for a week.

Other causes Caffeine can make breastfed babies irritable, so if you're breastfeeding, reduce your caffeine intake. Some babies have problems digesting the lactose in milk. Your doctor or health visitor will advise you.

The outlook Be reassured that babies with colic continue to eat and gain weight normally, despite the crying.

Comforting your older baby

Once you've learned to read your baby's cries, it becomes much easier to soothe him. As with young babies, older babies cry when they want attention, or are hungry or uncomfortable. However, as they develop, they may also cry because of frustration, boredom or fear of separation.

What you can do

If your usual techniques fail to comfort your baby, check these tips to see if there's something else you could try.

★ Enjoy a gentle sing-song, give him some time on your lap while you talk to him in baby language or sing a soothing lullaby to help quieten him.

★ Calm him down by holding or rocking him in your arms.

★ Try not to be anxious. Babies respond to the atmosphere in the room and your distress in kind.

★ Set up a routine so that he gets to know what to expect during the day. This can help him feel more secure and so calm him down.

Shift her attention Babies are easily distracted, and can be made to smile and laugh even when upset. Find a favourite toy and catch his attention. Or tickle him, play clapping games or sing to her. He'll be reassured by your happy mood.

TOP TIP
Try to be flexible and in tune with your baby's needs. If he's inexplicably upset, he may simply need the comfort of being held in your arms.

A quick response Leaving your baby to cry doesn't teach her anything but distrust. Secure babies are those who have their needs met, and have parents who respond to their cries, which is the only way they have to communicate.

A reassuring touch Patting your baby gently on her back and bottom can be enormously soothing. She may simply wish to know you're there, and will feel comforted by your presence.

Getting out Sometimes a change of scene is just what your baby needs, so get him out into the fresh air in his pushchair. Chances are the rhythmic movement will encourage him to doze off, or at least distract him enough to ease his crying.

Dealing with separation anxiety

This normal stage of development usually rears its head at about six or seven months of age, when your baby has developed a strong attachment to you as his primary carer. Not surprisingly, he can feel real distress when you need to be separated – even if it's just for a moment!

Let him know you'll return There is no need to try and avoid separations when your baby is young; he should get used to being with other people from time to time. You can try leaving the room for a couple of minutes and then reappearing, so he learns that you will always return.

Gradual introductions Let him get to know babysitters and carers before being left with them.

Provide transitional objects These help your baby to cope with separation. This could be a favourite teddy, blanket or an article of your clothing.

Comfort your baby Try not to make light of your baby's distress: comfort and reassure him. Try not to say "don't cry", which may make him feel like it's wrong to feel sad. Instead, say "I know you are sad. I love you. I'll be back soon." He may not understand much of what you're saying, but he'll feel reassured by your comforting tone.

Always say goodbye Disappearing will make your baby feel insecure, and he may spend much of his day looking for you, or wondering where you went. If you say goodbye, he'll soon understand that this means you are leaving and wave goodbye. Equally, however, he will also start to remember that you always come back.

A growing reluctance As your baby grows, she may resist being held by others. Get her used to new faces gradually.

Connecting through touch

Your baby's sense of touch is one of her most advanced senses at birth. As she develops, touch remains fundamental to her understanding of the world. Recognizing this, and connecting with her through touch, enhances her wellbeing and helps you enjoy the wonderful softness of your baby.

New sensations Your baby loves close contact with you. Experiment with different types of touch and let her experience new sensations as you blow a raspberry on her tummy, neck or feet. As she gets older, she'll giggle with delight.

  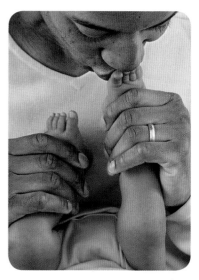

Keep eye contact When you're touching and massaging your baby, keep eye contact with her to help her feel safe and secure. Try "nesting" small babies on a towel to encourage them to look at you rather than turn their heads.

Regular touch Make touch a part of your everyday communication with your baby. Touch different parts of her body and face and name them as you do so, and sing action nursery rhymes that involve touch and physical interaction.

Feeling close Touching your baby is a great way to settle her, and to establish a close physical relationship. She'll feel loved and cared for, and you may find that you bond more easily and more deeply if you spend a little time exploring her body.

Your baby's comfort

When touching or massaging your baby (see pp.146–7), follow the guidelines below to ensure that the experience is a comfortable one for her and as relaxing as possible. Getting the basics of baby massage right helps to make touch a positive and important part of your relationship.

Do make sure that your baby is at least four weeks old. Look into her eyes and tell her what is happening so that she gets to know what to expect.

Do stop a massage if your baby objects and wait until she's feeling calmer.

Do always choose a time that is good for you and baby. If she's hungry or tired, or you are pressed for time, the experience will not be as rewarding.

Do make this a quiet time with no other distractions. All babies respond well to time alone with mum or dad, and you can take this opportunity to chat and sing to her, which will begin to spark her interpersonal skills. Turn off the television, radio and telephone, and enjoy this time with her. Let her get used to hearing your voice – and encourage her to respond with her own.

Do make sure you have everything you need within easy reach before starting a massage, such as nappies, spare clothing, warm oil, towels and cushions.

Do be careful when you finish a massage – your baby will be slippery!

Do make sure that she is on a safe surface and don't leave her unattended at any time. If your baby is small enough, you can sit on the floor and massage her on your lap. Otherwise, spread a towel on the floor or on any safe, raised surface.

Don't massage your baby if she is feeling unwell or just had immunisations.

Don't worry about "doing it right" – have fun! Use gentle rhythmic movements, and be guided by your baby as to what she enjoys or when she's uncomfortable.

Massaging your baby

Baby massage provides a wonderful way to spend time with your baby, getting to know his body and relax him at the same time. There is also plenty of evidence to suggest that baby massage offers a host of benefits for both you and your baby.

What you'll need

Be prepared before starting a massage; check that you have everything you need and that the environment is right.

★ Use a gentle massage oil, such as grapeseed, olive oil or apricot kernel oil, to help your hands glide over your baby's body.

★ When massaging hands and feet, you could use cushions or towels to prop him up so that he can see you.

★ Make sure the room is warm, quiet, and free of distractions.

★ Have clean nappies to hand for the end of the massage.

★ Have a change of clothing ready so that you can dress your baby promptly when you've finished.

TOP TIP
Try smearing a little of the oil you plan to use onto a small area of your baby's skin to check first for any allergic reactions. Avoid any nut-based oils.

Make it social While massaging your baby, keep contact with him through your voice and eyes as well as through touch. Smile at him and coo or sing to enhance the experience and help him feel relaxed.

1 Very gently stroke his face and head, moving away from his eyes. Massage his head as though you are shampooing his hair. Watch him relax as he responds to your soothing strokes.

2 Gently massage your baby's shoulders and upper back. Cup your hands over his shoulders with your fingers on his back and use gentle sweeps, strokes and circling movements.

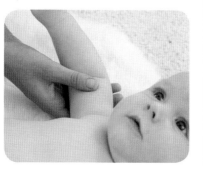

3 Massage his chest and abdomen using gentle strokes and moving in clockwise and counter-clockwise circles up and down his body.

4 Stroke his arms, pulling gently in a downwards motion. Keep eye contact all the time and smile, and coo at him as you touch his body.

5 Glide your hands down the front and back of one leg, then gently stroke it from the top to the bottom. Repeat on the other leg.

6 Massage his feet, which helps to relax his whole body. Using your thumbs, massage the sole with little circles. Play with and gently pull each toe.

The benefits of massage

Baby massage brings a host of benefits for both your baby and you, not least of which is that it can help to enhance your relationship.

Multiple benefits Studies have found that regular baby massage encourages bonding between parent and baby. It releases oxytocin and endorphins (the pain-relief hormones), which can relieve discomfort from teething and colic; improves sleep and encourages healthy weight gain; stimulates digestion; deepens respiration; tones muscles and aids growth; and even helps cognitive development by enhancing the rate at which your baby's neural cells "fire".

Reducing stress One UK study found that massaging a baby can help to build a better relationship between babies and mothers who have postnatal depression, and that massaged babies tend to cry less frequently, and sleep more soundly.

Winding down As well as the many benefits for your baby and for your relationship together, massaging your baby is also relaxing for you, helping you to unwind, which in turn improves your ability to cope.

Stimulating your baby

ENCOURAGING DEVELOPMENT

In just a year, your baby grows and develops dramatically, changing from a helpless newborn to an inquisitive, mobile baby, who responds to you and her world with enthusiasm and delight.

Your relationship with your baby will become stronger and more exciting as she begins to assert her personality and take her first steps on the road to independence.

The most important thing you can do to encourage your baby's development is to spend time with her. She will learn more from her relationship with you, and the activities you undertake together, than you may ever have imagined. Babies are wonderful mimics, and pick up everything from your tone of voice and your facial expressions, to the way you soothe her and even load your washing machine. She will increasingly want to be just like mum and dad, and copy your movements and your affection for one another.

THE IMPORTANCE OF PLAY

Play is a hugely important part of your baby's development on every level: social, emotional, physical and cognitive. In fact, what babies see, touch, hear and smell causes their brain connections to be made, especially if the experiences happen in a loving, consistent and predictable manner.

While there is a huge range of toys now available to stimulate your baby, all of which can be lots of fun to explore together, she will also learn a great deal from simple things, such as "chatting" with mum and dad, watching her siblings career about the house, taking a walk in the park and generally exploring the world around her.

As your baby's coordination develops, she will begin to enjoy playtime more than ever. Also, as her mobility increases, it may be hard to keep track of her as she manoeuvres her way around your home on a series of investigations. This is all part of her play.

BABY CHAT

Talking to your baby is an extremely important aspect of her development, and she will learn from both of you the subtle nuances of language as well as communication and interpersonal skills. Her first vocabulary will be dictated by how you speak to her and the words you use to

Keep talking Chat to your baby and hold her close. She loves the sound of your voice, and will soon instinctively respond with noises of her own!

Hide and seek See your baby's delight when she discovers that you're still there, even if she can't see you! Encouraging laughter also instils a wonderful sense of fun.

On the move A baby-proofed home leaves your mobile baby free to have fun. Let him explore his world, and discover how to reach and get the things that interest him.

describe things. Spending time with your baby, pointing out the things that make up her world, explaining the activities that you undertake together, and naming the colours that surround her, all help her to grasp the art of conversation and the meaning of words, as well as enhance her understanding.

If you run out of topics, don't worry about repeating yourself. Babies love the familiarity of repetition, and even very small ones absorb much more than you think!

COMMUNICATION

Don't underestimate the importance of communicating with your baby constantly. Communication involves far more than just words. Touch is an enormously powerful vehicle through which you can communicate with your baby – providing reassurance, security and comfort that go far beyond words. Chatting, making faces, teaching your baby signs, encouraging eye contact and even simply holding your baby close and feeding her, all represent lovely forms of communication that will encourage her development on all levels.

Your baby's world is expanding constantly, and everything you do with her will encourage healthy development, creativity, confidence and independence.

Stimulating play Toys encourage development and provide stimulation. Take time to show her how things work, then she can attempt them on her own.

Pictures and words Reading to your baby is a fantastic way to encourage a love of books, and to teach him about stories, words and pictures. Even very young babies enjoy being read to, finding comfort in your voice.

Baby talk

As your baby comes into contact with different sights, sounds and stimuli, he'll start to make sense of his world. Talk to him constantly to help his understanding. He'll be reassured and stimulated by your voice.

What you can do

Your can stimulate your baby's language development in a number of ways.

★ Take him on "visits" to different rooms in the home, and outside. Stop in front of mirrors, and show him a bird or a butterfly, or a fast-moving car, naming each thing you point out. Everything will be new to your baby, and he will be fascinated by the wealth of light, colour, movement and sound. He will also learn that everything around him has a name.

★ Sing or read silly rhymes and songs – this encourages an early appreciation and understanding of language.

★ Talk and sing to your baby; lullabies and playful tunes introduce your baby to the rhythm of language and speech.

★ Mimic your baby's coos and smiles, to encourage a rapport.

★ Involve him in "conversations"; respond to his sounds as if they're words.

★ Read as often as you can. He won't understand much at first, but he'll love the experience of being close to you, and will learn from the rhythm of your voice.

Early communications Hold your baby close to your face and make eye contact with him. Exaggerate your expressions as you communicate with him. He'll be fascinated by your "conversation" and may even join in with his own sounds!

Give a commentary Chat to your baby as you go about activities, explaining what you're doing, seeing and using. This makes activities fun; he'll love the interaction and will begin to absorb his first words.

First books Board books with lift-the-flaps are good entertainment. Books with faces, mirrors, animals and big, exaggerated pictures are all popular. You could make a bedtime story a part of your routine from the outset.

Language development

Your baby's language develops steadily from birth as he listens constantly and absorbs information from the world around him.

At birth Your baby is fascinated by new sounds, but may startle at unexpected or loud noises. He communicates his needs by crying.

0–3 months As your baby develops, he may turn his head when he hears your voice, and may recognize vocal patterns. He is soothed by low, calming speech, and smiles when he hears the fun in your voice, or sees you smile at him. He may learn to smile and make different cries for different needs.

4–6 months Your baby may learn to babble, using mainly consonants ("bbb" and "ddd", for example). He may enjoy things that make a noise, and make sounds of distress or unhappiness when he doesn't feel his needs are being met. By six months he may begin to use different vowel sounds.

7–12 months Your baby really listens to you when you speak to him, and may know his name. He'll enjoy hand and singing games, which encourage him to learn the rhythm of speech. He may learn his first words, and the appropriate noises to get your attention. Words will begin to mean something to him, but your tone of voice will mean much more!

The power of words There is plenty of research to suggest that playing with your baby, singing to her, and talking to her can encourage healthy cognitive development, and it also provides the bedrock for her budding social skills.

153

Interacting with your baby

A baby's first relationship is with her parents, and you'll teach her a lot by interacting with her positively – and constantly. As well as learning social skills from you, she'll develop her powers of language and learn to trust.

Behaviour and emotions

Interacting positively with your baby and offering encouragement and love, helps her to grow in confidence and learn to believe in herself and her abilities.

★ Always give positive feedback. Build your baby's confidence and enforce good behaviour patterns by responding positively to her achievements.

★ Talk about her feelings As she grows, this will help her to recognize what she's experiencing and to be confident expressing her emotions.

Reading together Reading to your baby and exploring books together is a wonderful form of interaction, employing both physical closeness and entertainment. You will also encourage a love of books in your baby.

Part of the fun Laugh with your baby, mimic her expressions and hold her close so that she feels engaged with you as you interact together. Teach her that communication is fun, and respond to her coos and smiles with your own.

Move to the music Sing and dance with your older baby, lift her high up in the air, and then swing her carefully about. She'll become involved in the music and movement, and will be enthralled by what her body can do!

I can do that too Smile at your baby and exaggerate your facial expressions; she will try, even very early on, to imitate them. In fact, your communication through the exchange of expressions will mark your first real "conversations" together.

Baby signing

Babies use all kinds of signs and gestures as a natural part of learning to talk. Encouraging your baby with extra signs for words like "milk", "more", "change nappy" or "tired" can help her to communicate before she speaks. You can make up your own signs, or use some recognized ones.

Introducing signs The ideal moment to introduce new signs is in a natural situation. Mealtimes are ideal for words such as "milk", "more", "drink" and "all gone". Above is the sign for "sleep".

Words and signs Always say and sign the word at the same time. Signing is not meant to replace language. Your baby will enjoy learning signs for favourite things, such as pets (such as the sign for "cat" above).

Clear expressions Use clear, lively facial expressions. Babies react to animated faces and clear gestures. Learning the sign for "milk", above, helps your baby let you know if she's hungry.

Encouraging social skills

Even the most naturally sociable baby can become wary of, and distressed by, strangers as they approach the six- or seven-month mark. However, with a few simple steps, you can encourage your baby to enjoy the company of other people and form strong relationships.

Supervising older children

While it can be tempting to leave a sibling in charge of your baby while you dash to the toilet or take a quick phone call, it's important not to leave them unsupervised.

Involving siblings Being overly cautious can undermine the sibling relationship, however, you must be vigilant at all times. Try giving siblings small tasks, such as stroking the baby's feet or tummy when he's upset, or fastening nappy tabs when you change him. Your older child will enjoy being involved.

A helping hand Much older children may be able to help out, changing nappies, giving feeds and even settling a baby down to sleep at times, but never assume knowledge. Teach older children how to care for your baby, and point out anything that could be a hazard. Show them how to hold him, and warn them about choking, scalding and tripping. Even older children need supervision until you're certain that they've grasped the basics.

Reassurance Hold all of your children together sometimes, so that each feels equally loved and valued.

Sibling play Although you must always supervise your baby with her siblings, it's equally important to allow them the space to form their own relationships. This may involve lots of giggling and silly play; as long as your baby is safe, it's a good idea to allow her to enjoy the fun.

Being confident If your baby is confident that you're in charge, she'll feel more secure in company. Be positive when you greet people: shake hands, kiss and hug and do whatever feels natural. These exchanges form the basis of her understanding of social skills.

Dads too Even if you're breastfeeding, it's important to encourage your partner to create a special role in your baby's life. Men offer a different insight into the world, and your baby will benefit from learning and playing in the company of his dad.

A special relationship The relationship that your baby has with his grandparents will be invaluable in years to come. He will learn a great deal from their experience, and benefit from their love. Encourage your parents to relate stories and sing rhymes and songs that will entertain your baby for hours.

Your baby's coordination

As the weeks and months pass, your baby will fine-tune her coordination skills as her developing brain makes sense of the world around her. There's plenty that you can do to encourage her coordination, and all of it is fun!

How coordination develops

When your baby is born, she reacts to her surroundings instinctively and is unable to control her movements. Over time, she loses her newborn reflexes and begins to move consciously.

★ At about two months, she'll exert more control over her limbs and may "cycle" her arms and legs when excited.

★ By three months, she may coordinate the movement of her hands and fingers a little better and enjoy clasping her hands together. You may also notice her making more coordinated movements with her arms and legs.

★ Between four and six months, your baby's balance and movement improve dramatically, as she begins to use and coordinate her large muscles. This helps her reach towards objects with both hands, and grasp at toys with her palms.

★ Between seven and nine months, she will develop leg and trunk coordination, sit alone steadily and may even begin to crawl using both of her hands and feet.

★ After nine months, your baby will develop more control over her hands and fingers and may be able to grab small objects with her forefinger and thumb. As her brain continues to grow, control over her large muscles is refined.

Taking a bat Your young baby will be mesmerized by the bright colours of a baby gym. At first she may be surprised when she bats one into action. She won't operate them herself until she's three or four months old.

Wrist rattles These make a satisfactory noise when your baby moves her arms, and help her learn to create a noise on purpose. Encouraging her to purposefully move parts of her body helps her coordination.

Exploring textures Soft, textured toys will enthral your baby, and she'll be surprised when she unexpectedly moves them or encourages them to make a sound. It will be many weeks before she is able to control her movements to make her toys respond.

Back and forth Hand your older baby a toy and encourage her to give it back. Watch as she lifts it to her mouth, and her look of surprise as she drops it. Engaging her in these activities helps to improve her coordination.

Cause and effect Toys that pop up or respond when your baby touches them are ideal for encouraging coordination skills as she'll be excited enough to try to make them work herself, even if it takes some time.

Fine movements Toys with buttons and dials provide endless entertainment for your older baby. These help her to become more adept with her hands as she learns to hit the right spots or turn the switches.

Messy play Making a mess is to be encouraged as your baby learns how things work by exploring her surroundings. Everything she does with her hands stimulates the part of the brain that governs coordination, and sensations of touch improve her cognition.

Turning pages Encourage your older baby to lift the flaps on board books, and turn the pages herself. Chunky, brightly coloured books are best, and those that make a sound when pressed will encourage her to try to make them respond to her own efforts.

Encouraging movement

Your baby will begin to explore the world around him as his coordination and mobility develops. Finding activities to test his muscles and strength encourages healthy development – and he'll love the new experiences.

Moving his arms Choose a baby gym with dangling bits that respond to even the lightest kick or "bat" from your baby. He will attempt to repeat the action himself, and learn that his excited movements have an astonishing response.

Tummy time Spending time on her front will help to develop your baby's neck muscles, by encouraging her to lift her head and look around. More importantly, it will excite her curiosity, and get her ready for crawling and rolling.

Reaching over Put toys just out of reach so that your older baby is encouraged to bend and reach out to get them. This improves his hand–eye coordination, and also helps to get him moving.

On the move Play crawling games with your baby. Chase her as she moves away and encourage her to crawl to you. Once your baby starts to crawl, a fully baby-proofed home is essential (see p.46).

Flying high Lift your baby in the air, and play airplanes, encouraging him to reach out his arms. He'll love becoming aware of how his body moves in different situations, and wriggle his muscles in excitement!

Cruising Holding onto furniture allows your baby to explore her new ability to stand upright. Arrange furniture so that she can move around. Over time, create spaces so that she can test her walking skills without feeling too pressured.

Learning to move

Some babies are intrepid travellers and will roll and shuffle before the six-month mark, while others are more cautious. You can, however, expect your baby to reach the following milestones.

From about three or four months When your baby's neck muscles become stronger, he may start to roll. Some babies flip themselves unexpectedly, but once they realize that they are capable of this new trick, they'll repeat it.

By six to seven months Your baby may be able to sit without support now. This is a precursor to crawling, as he leans forwards in a tripod position to hold his weight.

At six to eight months Many babies start to balance on their hands and knees, and often rock back and forth. From here, they learn how to move forwards and backwards by pushing off with their knees.

It's worth noting that some babies never crawl. Instead, they bottom shuffle, move on their tummies, or go straight to walking. It doesn't matter how your baby negotiates his space, as long as he moves. Tummy time (see left) helps to develop the muscles necessary to crawl.

Between nine and 13 months Your baby may show an interest in pulling himself up. It may take some time before he manages his first steps alone, but by 18 months, most babies are proficient walkers. It's not unusual for babies to learn quickly, either; some babies may go from first steps to running in a few short weeks!

Playtime with young babies

Playtime is more than entertainment. Your baby learns through play, and as her coordination and muscle control improves, she develops an awareness of her environment, of cause and effect, and the notion of security.

Playtime tips

Simple play will delight your baby. Play is crucial for your baby's social, emotional, physical, and cognitive development.

★ Play music that your baby seems to enjoy, and copy her reactions.

★ Choose toys that are tactile to encourage your baby to get familiar with lots of different physical experiences.

★ Teach her a variety of sounds by jingling keys, shaking a box of rice and knocking on the table. She'll soon turn her head to see what's going on.

★ Some babies are easily overstimulated. If your baby starts to cry during playtime, switch to calmer activities such as reading from a picture book, singing quietly or simply feeding.

Fun sensations Babies love to be tickled. Their sense of touch develops well before their motor skills and coordination, and they'll respond by about three months of age.

Peek-a-boo Play this favourite game with your hands, or hide your face briefly behind a towel or muslin square. Don't disappear for too long, or she'll forget you were there!

Visual stimulation Place a brightly coloured toy in front of her. Before she can move, she'll be fascinated by the colours, and as soon as possible, she will aim to reach out and touch it.

Action games Row your baby back and forth to show her different movements. When she's older, lift her arms, and play clapping games. She will love the fun and will attempt to mimic your actions.

Toys for young babies

Toys are not essential for your young baby, as there are many ways to stimulate and encourage her in everyday life. There are, though, many age-appropriate toys that can challenge and entertain her.

Bold patterns Black and white bold geometric shapes with clear outlines, brightly coloured, contrasting toys, or clear pictures or photos of faces will all appeal to your new baby.

Who's in the mirror? Babysafe mirrors will keep your baby occupied as she tries to identify her new friend. She won't recognize herself for a while, but she'll love to see the movement and light in the reflection.

Toy safety

Take care when choosing toys and follow the safety guidelines below.

★ **Read the labels** to check that toys are age-appropriate: they may have parts that pose a threat to your baby.

★ **Avoid toys with ribbons** that pose a strangulation risk, or teddies or dolls with beady eyes that could be choked on.

★ **Look for washable toys** that can be easily cleaned. Your little one will put everything in her mouth for months to come: if her toys become a bit grubby they may pose a threat to her health.

★ In the UK and the EU, a childsafe toy will be labelled with the kitemark EN71. Never purchase anything without this.

Play mats These provide a brilliant opportunity for your baby to experience some stimulating tummy time, which will help to build her neck muscles, and encourage her to explore her world.

Fabric picture books Soft fabric books encourage your baby to understand the concept of stories. As she develops, look out for interactive books with colourful pictures to stimulate her, and flaps to lift up.

Baby rattles These are ideal once your baby can confidently hold things and she'll love the fact that she can control it. If she's very little, wait – she may bang herself on the head one time too many!

Playtime for older babies

As your baby learns more about his world and develops the skills to move, he'll look for new stimulation. Parental interaction cannot be underestimated now, as his trust in you helps him feel confident in play.

Knocking down Your baby will enjoy swiping at towers of blocks and knocking them over. This type of activity is ideal for improving her hand–eye coordination. As she gets older, she will begin to show more interest in building herself, with your help.

Hide and seek Help your baby's cognitive development, problem-solving ability and memory by encouraging him to find a hidden toy. This also helps him grasp the concept of object permanence: that things still exist even when he can't see them.

Clapping games As your baby grows and develops, he'll become better at remembering and anticipating nursery rhymes and will have the manual dexterity to join in with clapping or actions. Sit facing him and encourage him to copy your actions.

Fun with mirrors Hold your baby in front of a mirror. She'll be fascinated by the "other" baby and will often smile at and talk to her new friend. She'll start to anticipate seeing this friendly baby each time she looks.

Read regularly Choose boards designed to be explored by little hands. Books that respond with sounds and music when touched can also be popular, as your baby learns that he can control things himself.

Pointing out Take your baby on a tour of your home, providing her with words for everything you come across. Your baby will be fascinated by all these new things, and you'll be helping her language development.

Toys for older babies

Now that your baby can sit unsupported, he will be able to sustain play activities for longer. Give him toys that consolidate and challenge his improved hand–eye coordination skills and cognitive development.

First puzzles These are easy to assemble. Assist him at first, and he'll soon understand what has to be done! If he becomes impatient, help him out. It's better that he knows that he can get the job done with a little perseverance than just to give up.

Stacking cups Your older baby is starting to enjoy putting things together. Different sized plastic cups are great fun now, and introduce him to the concepts of bigger and smaller. Ones with holes in the bottom double up as "pouring" cups for bathtime.

Musical fun Simple instruments are a fantastic way to keep your baby entertained, and encourage his understanding of music, but don't expect anything tuneful! Let him bang away so that he understands that every stroke does something different.

Sandy play Everything that your baby plays with helps him get to grips with how things work. A sandbox is ideal, encouraging him to pour, sift, build and create in one little space. Wait until your baby has passed the everything-in-the-mouth stage, though.

Staying safe

As well as shop-bought toys, your baby will enjoy playing with and exploring everyday household objects. Your job is to ensure that everything he comes into contact with is safe for him to handle.

Safe to suck Check that any kitchen items that double up as playthings, such as sieves and plastic containers, have no sharp edges that could hurt your baby if he put them into his mouth. Keep checking old yogurt pots and other plastic items to ensure they're not cracked, and dispose of them as soon as they become damaged.

Hazardous substances Beware of the risk of poisoning. Don't give your baby an empty plastic bottle that originally contained a substance that could have harmed him, such as a cleaning fluid. Even if you've washed it out, there may still be some residue remaining.

Avoid heavy items Don't give your baby anything heavy to play with that could hurt him if he dropped it on his foot, hand or head.

Outings and lifestyle

GETTING OUT AND ABOUT

Once you've settled in at home with your new baby and have mastered the basics of babycare, you'll enjoy the opportunity to take your new arrival out and about, to plan family outings together and to resume a more active lifestyle once more.

Having a new baby in the family will obviously change the family dynamic as well as the way you operate on a day-to-day basis. However, as your baby grows and develops, and you become more accustomed to her everyday care, you'll begin to find it easier to manage, which will in turn help you to relax and really start to explore and enjoy the opportunities that family life presents. The arrival of your new baby is a wonderful time to establish regular family outings, start a tradition of family holidays and perhaps enjoy a more active, outdoors life than you did previously. We'll look at ways to make the transition from couple to family easier, as you begin to incorporate new, family-oriented activities into your lifestyle.

Make the most of your maternity and paternity leave to enjoy this time with your baby, and make sure you spend quality time all together as a family whenever possible.

SAFETY FIRST

As always, it's crucial to consider the safety of your baby once you start to venture a little further afield. Choosing the right travel equipment to keep your baby safe in every eventuality is an important starting point, and in this chapter we'll look at everything you need to know to keep your baby as safe and comfortable as possible while travelling, whether on short trips in her buggy, or on longer journeys.

A HEALTHY LIFESTYLE

It's worth reminding yourself that you are your baby's first teacher, and that the lifestyle you lead will influence her and encourage her to develop her own good habits and help her understanding of the world. Eating well, getting out into the fresh air, exercising regularly and establishing a happy family environment will all teach your baby about the importance of healthy living and the joys of family life and relationships, and will set her in good stead for many years to come.

Everything that you do with your baby will have an impact on her emotional and physical health and wellbeing, so we'll look at the best ways to achieve a balanced, healthy lifestyle and diet that in turn encourages her to thrive.

MAKING DECISIONS

The time will soon come when you will have to make some decisions about your future, or decide whether you're still happy with the plans you've made. Will you choose to stay at home with your baby or return to work on a full- or part-time basis?

A dose of fresh air Your baby will love getting out into the fresh air, and will soon accept it as part of his daily routine. Sunlight helps to ensure that he gets the vitamin D he needs for healthy bones, teeth and immunity, and, once he's mobile, the exercise he gets will make him physically tired enough to sleep well.

The prospect of going back to work can be a daunting one, and you may be concerned about how to juggle the various elements of your life, and get the best possible childcare for your baby. It's important to recognize that your priorities change dramatically when you become a parent. It can therefore be helpful to sit down with your partner and work out what matters to you both most, now that you are a family.

Later in this chapter, we'll look at the best ways to ensure your family's wellbeing, whether you decide to return to work, stay at home or share the care of your baby with your partner.

YOUR NEW LIFE TOGETHER

Most importantly, however, this chapter is about celebrating your life with your wonderful new baby and creating the family life that you want as your horizons expand.

Resuming exercise Taking some time for yourself to resume your fitness habits will make you better able to cope with the many demands of parenting.

Back to work Establishing a strong relationship with your baby's babysitter or carer will make the process of going back to work that much easier.

Family holidays Travelling with your baby can be great fun, as you introduce her to a host of new sights, smells and experiences. She'll soon become as intrepid as you are!

Your baby's car seat

The most important thing to consider when buying a car seat is your baby's safety, and the practicality of the seat. Your baby will grow quickly and his seat will need replacing within months, so consider your budget.

What you need to know

Be aware of the latest recommendations and safety advice before purchasing and using your baby's car seat.

★ When you purchase a car seat, get the shop to show you how to fit it properly. Many car seats are fiddly to fit correctly, so it's important to get advice to ensure that it's fitted safely.

★ A new child restraint system called ISOFIX has been introduced. ISOFIX points are fixed connectors in a car's structure into which an ISOFIX child seat can be plugged. Check the seat and your car's manufacturer's manual to be sure that both your car and the seat are compatible with this system.

★ Experts recommend that you do not use a second-hand car seat.

★ Always ensure that your car seat meets the latest safety standard, and has a British or European kitemark: ECE R44.03 or R44.04.

Easily transportable Your baby's car seat acts as a temporary seat for him when you're out and about, and allows you to transport him from the car to your home without disturbing him if he's fallen asleep.

Fitting the car seat The safest position for your baby's first car seat is rear-facing in the back of the car. Ensure that it is fitted properly. For the first few outings, you may wish to sit in the back with him to get him used to it.

Strapped in securely Your baby's car seat needs a secure harness to keep him safe. Choose a seat with an easy-to-fasten harness so you can get him in and out quickly if necessary – and don't forget to fasten it! The safest type of harness is a five-point one, with straps both over your baby's shoulders and between his legs.

Stress-free journeys

As your baby grows, you may find that he's more alert during car journeys and demands a greater degree of attention. Try some simple techniques to keep him soothed and entertained in the car.

Music and songs A CD with favourite children's songs and rhymes can soothe as well as entertain.

A favourite toy Babies often fall asleep in cars. Bring a spare "comforter", such as a soft toy, if your older baby needs one to fall asleep.

Activity centres Ideal for older babies, these strap onto the seat facing your baby to provide a fun distraction. You

can also purchase a mini-baby gym to hang from the handle of his car seat, which he can bat and handle.

Keep talking Chat to your baby, and encourage him to look out of the window at trees, clouds and birds.

Your baby's comfort A sunshade fixed firmly to the window keeps the sun off your baby. Some have patterns on the inside to attract his attention.

Car entertainment Toys that attach to your baby's seat can distract and occupy him on longer journeys.

Baby slings

Slings are great for hands-free activities, and for going out without a big piece of equipment. Your baby will feel reassured being held close to you.

Chest slings These are best for new babies as they offer sufficient support for the head and neck. Make sure that your partner comes along to try out the sling before buying it if you both plan to use it.

Ensuring comfort If you plan to use your sling a lot, look for one with padding and sturdy, wide shoulder straps. This will not only be more comfortable, but will take the pressure off your back.

Carrying older babies Looser, hammock-style slings are good for transporting older babies who have stronger head and neck muscles and so are able to hold their heads upright unsupported.

Backpacks Older babies enjoy being carried in a knapsack-style sling on your back. Look for one with good back support and that allows you to adjust the seat to make it narrower for smaller babies.

Sling safety

There have been recent safety concerns about carrying young babies in pouch-style slings. Being informed limits the risks.

Suffocation risks Slings can pose breathing hazards to babies. In the first months, babies' weak neck muscles mean they can't control their heads. If fabric presses against your baby's nose and mouth, she cannot move away. Hammock-type slings that keep your baby in a curled position bend her chin to her chest, restricting her airway and limiting her oxygen supply.

Safety tips It's now recommended that parents ensure that their baby's face is not covered, and is visible at all times. If you're breastfeeding your baby in a sling, change her position after a feed so that her head is facing up and is clear of both the sling and your body. For young babies, use an upright sling that provides neck support and check your baby frequently while she's in a sling.

Safety standards Check that a sling carrier has the British Standards Institute (BSI) safety number: BS EN 13209 Part 2:2005.

Facing out As your baby grows and develops and her neck muscles become stronger, you will be able to carry her facing outwards in her sling. This will satisfy her growing curiosity about the world.

Pushchairs and buggies

A pushchair or buggy will be one of your biggest baby purchases, so choose one that suits you and your lifestyle. Test-drive it to ensure that the handle is the right height, the brake is easy to use, and it's manageable.

Choosing a pushchair or buggy

Before choosing your baby's pushchair or buggy, consider the following:

★ Do you want a convertible pushchair that reclines fully for a newborn baby, and then converts to a buggy when your baby can sit up? Or do you want to have a carrycot attachment, so your baby can sleep lying flat while you're out?

★ Do you want your baby to face you or outwards? He'll be reassured by your face when he's small, and you will need easy access to him. When he's older, he'll want to see where he's going.

★ Choose a pushchair or buggy that carries the BSI safety number: BS EN 1888:2003 and European safety standards number EN1888.

★ Look for good suspension and large wheels to give a more comfortable ride.

★ Ensure the model has a five-point safety harness that can be adjusted for your baby's size, and opened quickly.

★ Check that the height is right for you; some have adjustable handles for taller family members.

★ Make sure a pushchair fits in the car, is light enough to carry, and easy to fold.

★ There should be two locking systems on your baby's pushchair: one can be released to collapse the pushchair, while one stays activated to prevent the pushchair from collapsing straightaway. This prevents you from accidentally enfolding your baby in the chair.

Newborn pram There's a wide variety of pushchairs for newborns, all of which allow your baby to lie flat. A carrycot can be lifted off the chassis so that your baby can remain sleeping in it when indoors.

An adjustable buggy At around six months, your baby will want to sit up. Many newborn buggies have adaptable settings to allow this. Modern buggies often have higher seats, so that getting your baby in and out is easier.

Travel system 2-in-1 or 3-in-1 travel systems combine a carrycot, pushchair, and sometimes a car seat, in one system, enabling you transfer your baby between your car and home with little disturbance.

Braking Choose a pushchair that has brake pedals that are easy to turn on and off. Individual pedals can be preferable to a single bar that you could get caught on your foot or elsewhere.

Operating your buggy Ask for a demonstration on folding and unfolding your pushchair or buggy and on the use of the brake. Practise operating it a few times before you get your baby on board.

Strollers An easily operated, lightweight stroller for older babies can be ideal for quick trips out and holidays, being compact and easily transportable. They are also convenient to use on public transport.

Buggy accessories Check out which accessories are included. You'll need rain covers and a cosy blanket. You may also want a parasol for sun protection. Toys that attach to the buggy are handy too.

Transporting two

If you have twins, or another young child close in age to your baby, you will need to find a buggy or pushchair to accommodate them both together.

Think about your requirements when choosing a model – where will you be using it and does it suit the different needs of both your children?

What to consider As with single buggies, you need to think about how you will be using your double buggy. If you'll be doing a lot of walking, check that the buggy is relatively light, and easy to manoeuvre and operate. If you need to get it in and out of the car a lot, it needs to be suitably compact, or if you use public transport, it needs to be manageable on buses and trains. Whatever you choose, test-drive a buggy before you purchase it.

Side-by-side buggies These can be difficult to operate in smaller spaces so consider how impractical this might be, for example, if you have narrow pavements to negotiate. Check too that

it will fit through standard doorways. On the plus side, they are usually fairly light and have adaptable seats, which can lie flat for newborns and can be raised as your babies grow. Another advantage of a side-by-side twin buggy is that both babies will have the same unobstructed view.

Different needs A tandem buggy, with one seat behind the other, is ideal for children of different ages as one seat usually reclines fully to accommodate a newborn, while the other seat is more upright for an older child. However, these can be difficult to use on public transport and, without help, stairs are tricky to negotiate. If your older baby is happy to stand, a buggy board attachment is an alternative.

Twin buggies Side-by-side buggies tend to be lightweight and easy to manage. Your twins, or young children, can also enjoy each other's company.

Your first outings

Your first trips out with your baby provide a welcome opportunity to get some fresh air. Prepare everything that you might need in advance to ensure that outings with your baby run smoothly!

Ready to go It's a good idea to keep your changing bag fully stocked and ready to go. It takes long enough to get a baby ready for an outing without searching for changing bag essentials at the last minute.

Dress for the weather Dress your baby appropriately for the weather, with a blanket and a hat to keep her warm if it's cold. Don't overdress her, though; she'll feel the heat as much as you when the weather is warm.

Travelling light In the early days and weeks, it's relatively easy to pop your baby into her sling and enjoy quick outings, keeping your hands free to carry light shopping or browse in a shop.

Be prepared Your baby may need changing at any point in your journey, so come prepared with everything you need to do this quickly and efficiently. A portable or disposable changing mat is a must.

Feeding in public You may feel odd at first breastfeeding in public, but as your confidence grows, you'll soon find that it's easy to feed discreetly when you're out. It's also incredibly convenient to be able to feed your baby anywhere at a moment's notice.

Being prepared

You may feel as though you've packed for an expedition when you leave your home, but the truth is that babies do require quite a bit of paraphernalia. It's worth bringing along the following essentials to avoid being caught out.

★ Your changing bag (see p.16), with several clean nappies, wipes and plastic bags for wet or dirty clothes or nappies.

★ A flannel, for emergency all-over washes.

★ A change of clothes; nappy explosions and possetting can both take their toll.

★ A couple of boxes of ready-prepared formula if you're bottle feeding, plus sterilized bottles with lids.

★ Muslin squares for mopping up.

★ A spare dummy or two, kept in a clean plastic bag.

★ A spare hat, jumper or coat for your baby, as well as a blanket.

★ Your camera and mobile telephone; consider a disposable camera that you can keep in your changing bag to catch those priceless first moments.

★ Small toys to distract your baby when she becomes bored or distressed.

★ A clean top for you.

★ A bottle of water for you, as well as some snacks: new parenthood demands a lot of energy!

TOP TIP

If your pushchair has good storage, keep a supply of baby essentials in it at all times. Shopping can be stored, too, but don't hang heavy bags from the handles as this can cause the buggy to tip back.

Short outings Even a short walk in your local park or a trip to the local shops can lift your spirits and add a little variety to your daily routine. Better still, make outings a regular part of family life.

Outings with your older baby

As your baby grows and develops and becomes increasingly mobile, he'll be able to enjoy plenty of exciting new activities. Introducing him to a range of situations and experiences will stimulate him and also help to develop his social skills.

Staying safe outdoors

Once your baby is more mobile, he'll enjoy the challenge of new activities in different environments. Be vigilant and aware of different hazards when he is playing away from home.

★ Go to the fenced off playground areas in parks, where your baby can sit and crawl safe from dogs.

★ Always supervise your baby near any water.

★ In parks and open spaces be on the lookout for hazards such as broken glass and dog mess.

★ Watch your baby at all times in a playground. Once he's mobile, whether crawling or walking, he may move quickly close to hazards such as moving swings or roundabouts.

★ Never let your baby play alone outdoors, even in your own garden.

Water babies Babies can swim in public pools from any age, although you may want to wait until she has good head control first. Introducing her to swimming early will make her more confident in the water.

On the swings A simple trip to the park can be a magical experience for your baby, especially once she is old enough to enjoy the playground equipment.

Meeting others Playgroups will give you the opportunity to chat to other mums while your little one tries out new toys, activities – and, eventually, friendships!

The mums' network Getting together with other mums, perhaps from your antenatal or postnatal group, offers a wonderful opportunity for your baby to socialize, and you'll enjoy exchanging stories and advice.

Top baby destinations

The more active your baby becomes, the more variety he'll enjoy when it comes to new places and activities.

Local park Your local playground provides perfect play opportunities for your older baby. Push him on the swings and let him crawl in the grass or the sandpit: pack buckets and spades for sandcastles. Take a rug to sit on, and enjoy summer picnics.

Playgroup Find out about local playgroups and visit regularly. Your baby will get to play alongside other babies and experiment with activities that you may not do often at home.

Children's farms Small zoos and farms geared towards young children provide a totally new experience. Many offer supervised petting of small animals and opportunities to feed farm animals as well as providing playground equipment.

Family or friends' homes For a change of scene, visit family or friends. Your inquisitive baby will be fascinated by the new environment and keen to explore. Keep an eye out for safety hazards (see pp.46–7).

Nature spots A walk by the river, feeding ducks at the pond, or a stroll in the woods all give your baby new sights and sounds to enjoy.

Shopping trips Make an outing of a trip to the local shops. Get your baby involved by giving him a purchase to hold and let him look at and handle fruit and vegetables before you put them in the trolley.

Staying healthy

With a new baby in the house, you have even more reason to stay fit and well. Making healthy leisure activities a part of your daily life will instil good habits in your baby that will last her a lifetime.

A nutritious diet

Continuing a healthy diet after the birth provides your baby with essential nutrients from your milk and helps you cope with the demands of parenthood.

★ Your postnatal and breastfeeding diet should be based around good-quality proteins, healthy fats, wholegrains and plenty of fruit and vegetables. These provide you with the nutrients that both you and your baby need to stay healthy and strong.

★ Don't be tempted to diet when you are breastfeeding: you'll need additional calories to feed your baby. With regular exercise, a healthy diet and exclusive breastfeeding, your baby weight will soon vanish.

★ Eat little and often and drink plenty of fresh water to keep your energy levels up.

A family picnic Make healthy eating a natural and fun part of your baby's world. Enjoy a family picnic together with lots of healthy snacks. Getting out regularly also teaches him the joys of an active lifestyle. Run, play and have fun in the sun.

Avoiding alcohol Drinking alcohol when breastfeeding isn't ideal as even a small amount makes its way into your milk. If you have the occasional drink, wait an hour or so before feeding your baby.

Exercising after the birth

It's important to take a sensible approach and start slowly and gently when beginning to exercise again.

Pelvic floor exercises You can practise these in the days and weeks after the birth: squeeze in your pelvic floor muscles (as if you were trying to stop your flow of urine midstream) and hold for a few seconds.

Tummy toners You may be tempted to do these immediately to regain your pre-pregnancy shape, but it's best to wait a few weeks after a normal birth, and for a minimum of six weeks after a Caesarean before doing any sit-ups or tummy exercises. Gentle exercise, such as walking, can be done earlier.

Gentle stretching This is ideal for the first six weeks or so after a normal birth. Don't join an exercise class unless it's designed for the postnatal period – your body needs sufficient time to recover, and if you exercise too soon you risk injuring yourself.

Swimming Exercising in water is an excellent way to tone up, but you should avoid swimming for at least seven days after your postnatal bleeding has stopped or – if you have had stitches or a Caesarean – until after your six-week check.

Exercising with your baby

These yoga stretches can be practised about six weeks after a normal birth, or eight weeks after a Caesarean. The sitting poses shown here help to strengthen the lower back and hips. Breathe through the poses and increase stretches gradually. Always stop if you feel any discomfort.

Simple twist Sit with both legs facing forwards, back straight and feet upwards. Bend your left knee, then cup your right arm around the left knee. Put your left hand behind you and gently turn. Repeat on the other side.

Forwards bend Sit upright with your legs extended forwards and back straight. Raise both arms, breathe in, then on an exhalation bend from the hips and extend forwards, stretching your hands towards your toes. Keep your legs straight and chest open.

Twisting forwards bend Sit tall. Bring your right leg under your left leg, then your left knee over your right. Raise the arms, join your palms, and extend forwards, keeping your back straight. Repeat with the opposite leg cross.

Food for fuel Parenting can be exhausting work, so make sure you have a varied, nutritious diet to keep your energy levels high. Babies are great mimics, and if they see you eating well, they'll want to do the same themselves.

An invigorating walk Taking your baby out for a daily walk in her buggy not only gives her fresh air and a change of scene, but also gives you the chance to work some exercise into your day, providing both a physical and a mental boost.

Going on holiday

Your first holiday with your baby may be a little daunting; however, being well-prepared and taking things at a pace that suits both you and your baby, will make the experience memorable for all the right reasons.

What you'll need

Depending upon the length of your journey and your destination, you may want to consider bringing the following:

★ **Nappies:** allow plenty for the time you are in transit, plus a few extras. You can usually buy more at your destination, but pack enough for two days just in case.

★ **Wipes, barrier cream,** baby bath and any other baby toiletries.

★ **Plastic bags** for dirty nappies, clothes and bibs.

★ Three to four spare dummies

★ Your baby's usual blanket

★ A travel cot with his usual bedding.

★ **Clothing:** one to two outfits a day. Cotton layers are ideal; include socks, jumpers or jackets in colder months.

★ Washable or disposable bibs

★ A small bottle of your baby's usual **laundry detergent** for emergency washes.

★ Sunscreen and a sunhat

★ Two to three hooded towels

★ If you're bottle-feeding, a supply of your baby's usual formula, and bottles, a bottle brush, teats and sterilizing tablets.

★ Your baby's transport. A sling for younger babies is convenient, or a light, foldable stroller for older babies.

★ A car seat for trains, buses, planes, cars and taxis at your destination.

★ A changing bag with a changing mat.

★ An extra shirt for yourself in your hand luggage for breast or baby leaks!

Your baby's first passport Don't forget to apply for your baby's passport! You can apply for this as soon as you have his birth certificate. This means that you'll be free to travel whenever you like.

Comfortable flying As well as being convenient while travelling, breastfeeding during the ascent and descent of an aeroplane helps to ease the pressure – and potential discomfort – on your baby's ears.

A supply of fluids In hotter climates, it's important to keep your baby well hydrated. Carry several bottles of previously boiled, cooled water for bottle-fed babies, or breastfeed your baby as often as he needs.

Sun protection Cover your baby and use sunscreen. Look for one with an SPF of at least 50 in a gentle cream designed for babies. Apply it often, particularly if she's been for a swim. And don't forget her hat!

A safe holiday

Checking in advance that your holiday destination is suitable for your baby is essential. Follow the guidelines below to ensure a safe and relaxing trip.

Choose family-friendly resorts
Holiday destinations that cater for families will be set up to ensure your baby's safety, and will be more likely to have the equipment and facilities you need to change your baby, allow him to sleep undisturbed and feed him when you need to.

Check facilities in advance Find out what facilities are provided. Some travel companies arrange for you to hire car seats, pushchairs and travel cots at your destination to save you taking a trailer-load of equipment. Will you be able to buy nappies or your baby's usual formula? Is there a doctor if your baby becomes ill? Are there babysitting facilities, and are the staff who undertake this job fully trained? Will a cot and bedding be provided? Is a hotel quiet enough for your baby to sleep during the day and at night, and are there parents' rooms with changing facilities?

Be prepared Include your baby on your travel insurance. Take any regular medication he needs. If he is eating solids, consider whether there will be appropriate meals at local restaurants, or places to buy baby food. If you're breastfeeding, avoid anything that could be a potential source of food poisoning.

Constant supervision Always watch your baby carefully when you are by water of any description.

Keep it simple The best holidays with babies and young children are uncomplicated ones. Simple beach holidays with a minimum of travelling around will be relaxing for you and plenty of fun for your baby.

Returning to work

Even if you enjoy your career, you'll no doubt feel some sadness at the prospect of returning to work and leaving your baby. Ensuring that you have good, reliable childcare makes the process that much easier.

Getting ready

Prepare your return to work carefully to reduce the stress involved.

★ **Line up your childcare** well in advance, and have several trial sessions. If your baby is used to her new routine, she will find it easier when you return to work.

★ **Find out in advance about part-time or flexible working,** and whether you have employment rights as a new parent.

★ **Going back to work doesn't have to mean giving up breastfeeding.** Find out whether you can have access to a quiet place and a fridge so you can express while you're at work.

★ **Make contact with your boss and colleagues** a week or so before you return to get to grips with what has been going on in your absence.

★ **Establish guidelines.** You may once have been a 24-hour-a-day employee, but that's no longer possible. If everyone knows where you stand at the outset, it's less likely that resentment will breed.

TOP TIP
Juggling a baby, a home and a job can be exhausting so make sure you take regular breaks, drink plenty of water, and eat healthily. Don't try to be superwoman!

Interviewing a nanny It's usual to interview a prospective nanny in your own home. Prepare your questions in advance and take notes. As well as asking him or her about his or her childcare approaches, ask for the details of referees too and contact them.

Choosing a nursery A good nursery will offer a stimulating and nurturing environment for your baby. Visit a few local nurseries to see how they operate, and use common sense and your instincts when making your decision.

Using a childminder These can offer the best of both worlds, providing the stimulation of other children, and a warm, family environment. A good childminder is usually booked up well in advance, so you will need to begin your search early.

At-home dads It may make sense for your partner to stay at home and take on the care of your baby. Many dads find it a rewarding experience. Make sure you're supportive and appreciative, even if you are perhaps a little jealous too!

Family care Grandparents may be in a position to offer childcare, which can be a wonderful arrangement. Your baby and his grandparents will benefit from the close relationship, and you'll be secure in the knowledge that he is in loving hands.

Choosing childcare

There are a variety of childcare options, including nannies, childminders and nurseries. Consider the pros and cons of each carefully.

Your needs Make a decision based on cost implications and what suits your working hours and lifestyle. You may find that you can adjust your hours to work more flexibly, or that you or your partner can go part-time to cut down the costs and spend more time with your baby.

Be meticulous Whatever childcare option you choose, check references, and, if possible, get a personal recommendation. Visit facilities and interview the staff. Ask how your baby will be spending her day, and how her needs will be met. How much attention will she get, and will she have a designated carer? Are the staff experienced? Are there babies of a similar age? Are the facilities clean, and will your baby have a quiet place to sleep? Check their fire exits and emergency procedures.

If you opt for a childminder, choose one who is registered, checked by the Criminal Records Bureau (CRB) properly insured, and trained in first aid. Your local authority has a list of registered childminders. Agencies are legally required to run CRB checks on their nannies.

Trust your instincts If a nursery or childminder ticks all the right boxes, has a similar approach to childcare as you do, and comes complete with fantastic references, then all should be well. If you don't feel comfortable, then look elsewhere.

The right balance

Being a parent can be a juggling act at times, whether or not you return to work. Establishing the right balance between work and family time can take off some of the pressure and ensure a fulfilling family life.

Full-time mum Staying at home gives you the chance to see your baby develop before your eyes. Get a break from time to time though, and try to involve your baby in your daily routine.

Back at work There is no reason why you can't be a great mum and employee once you learn to juggle the roles. Check in with your carer frequently to keep up to date with how your baby is doing.

Quality time As a working mum, you may have less time with your baby, but you can make each second count. Establish a routine so you're always there for a morning cuddle or the bedtime bath.

An evening breastfeed Even if you're unable to breastfeed your baby in the day, you can still produce enough milk to give him a comforting evening feed. You'll both enjoy this special time.

A good start to the day Sitting down to breakfast with your baby will reassure you that his day has started well, and you can chat and play games together while he is happy and alert.

Finding a babysitter

When you do get out with your partner, you'll want to know that you are leaving your baby in good hands.

Get a recommendation Choose a babysitter who has a personal recommendation and references, and follow them up.

Check experience Make sure he or she has dealt with babies, and knows what to do in an emergency. Ideally, your babysitter should have a first-aid certificate (or have taken a babysitting course).

Introduce everyone Your baby needs to meet the babysitter in advance. Even if he will be sleeping while you're out, he may be distressed to find an unfamiliar face if he wakes.

Explain your baby's routine Give your babysitter ideas for dealing with your baby if he wakes up. Make sure your sitter knows how to feed and change him, and settle him in bed.

Time for each other Getting out with your partner helps you to nurture your relationship and provide love and support for each other.

Useful resources

BREASTFEEDING
Association of Breastfeeding Mothers
www.abm.me.uk
08444 122 949

Breastfeeding Network
www.breastfeedingnetwork.org.uk
0300 100 0210

National Breastfeeding Helpline
www.breastfeeding.nhs.uk
0300 100 0212

La Leche League
www.laleche.org.uk
0845 120 2918

Ask a Midwife
www.midwivesonline.com
01274 427132

National Childbirth Trust
www.nct.org.uk
0300 33 00 771

BABY HEALTH AND SAFETY
Action for Sick Children
www.actionforsickchildren.org
0800 074 4519

Bliss
support for families of premature
and special care babies
www.bliss.org.uk
0500 618140

British Red Cross
www.redcross.org.uk
0844 871 1111

Child Accident Prevention Trust
www.capt.org.uk
020 7608 3828

Foundation for the Study of Infant Deaths
www.sids.org.uk
0808 802 6868

National Eczema Society
www.eczema.org
0870 241 3604

National Meningitis Trust
www.meningitis-trust.org
0800 028 1828

NSPCC
www.nspcc.org.uk
0808 800 5000

NEW MOTHERS
Association for Postnatal Illness
www.apni.org
020 7386 0868

Family Planning Association
www.fpa.org.uk
0845 122 8690

Pelvic Partnership
www.pelvicpartnership.org.uk
01235 820 921

Guild of Pregnancy and Postnatal Exercise Teachers
www.postnatalexercise.co.uk

Relate
www.relate.org.uk
0845 456 1310

Cry-sis
support for parents dealing with excessive crying
www.cry-sis.org.uk
08451 228 669

NAPPIES
National Association of Nappy Services
www.changeanappy.co.uk
0121 693 4949

Women's Environmental Network
www.wen.org.uk
020 7481 9004

CHILDCARE
Childcare Directory
www.childcaredirectory.co.uk
01379 898 535

Childcare Link
www.childcarelink.gov.uk

Daycare Trust
www.daycaretrust.org.uk
0845 872 6251

National Childminding Association
www.ncma.org.uk
0800 169 4486

Parents at Work
www.parentsatwork.org.uk
020 7628 3565

Working Families
www.workingfamilies.org.uk

Rights and benefits
Citizens Advice
www.citizensadvice.org.uk

DirectgovTax Credit help
www.direct.gov.uk
0845 300 3900

HMRC Child Benefit help
www.hmrc.gov.uk
0845 302 1444

Inland Revenue Tax Credit help
www.taxcredits.inlandrevenue.gov.uk
0845 300 3900

Working Families
www.workingfamilies.org.uk
020 7253 7243

GENERAL
Adoption UK
www.adoptionuk.org
0844 848 7900

Gingerbread
advice and information for one-parent families
www.gingerbread.org.uk
0800 018 5026

Home Start
support for families in local communities
www.home-start.org.uk
0800 0686 368

NHS Direct
nhsdirect.nhs.uk
0845 4647

Parentline Plus
ww.parentlineplus.org.uk
0808 800 2222

TAMBA (Twins and multiple birth association)
www.tamba.org.uk
0800 138 0509

Index

Acknowledgments

AUTHOR'S ACKNOWLEDGMENTS:

I am indebted to my husband Michael for his unstinting support and encouragement. I have been inspired in writing this book by my children and grandchildren, not forgetting my son and daughter in-law. I would also like to thank Karen Sullivan, the consultant editor, for her help and hard work, and everyone at DK who made the book possible, especially Claire Cross and Hannah Moore, Sarah Ponder, Mandy Lebentz, Penny Warren, Glenda Fisher and Peggy Vance.

PUBLISHER'S ACKNOWLEDGMENTS:

DK would like to thank Sara Kimmins for the initial idea and styling of books in the series; Becky Alexander for proofreading; Susan Bosanko for the index; Jo Godfrey-Wood for assistance at photo shoots; Victoria Barnes and Roisin Donaghy for hair and make-up; Carly Churchill, the photographer's assistant, and our models: Alice and Marlene Bowden; Louise and Caya Buckens; Kirsty and Kate Campbell; Giovanna Franchina and Leonardo Diallo; Leigh and Isla Haynes; Zara Hooley; Carrie Love and Dylan Tannazi; Cindy Arianne and Rhaya O'Donnell; Michelle and Edward Phillips; Hayley and Freya Sherwood; Michelle Streeting and Jasmine Wild; Georgia Suttling and Axl Habanananda; Mary Thomas and Tom Hartup; Karolina and Khemilya Ubor; Cordelia Bugeja and Luke and Eli Vyner; Victoria Wallace and Manny Watson; Danielle Valliere and Tom and Dylan Baird; Natasha Garry and Solstice River Davies; Lisa Crowe and Luca Sodeau; Karlyn and Darcy Westwood; Sabrina and Olivier Taylor; Marcella Woods and Michael-Gabriel Fiori-Woods; and Tessa Evans and Sassy Devonshire.

The publisher would like to thank the following for their kind permission to reproduce their photographs:

(Key: a-above; b-below/bottom; c-centre; l-left; r-right; t-top)

23 **Getty Images:** LWA (ca). **Science Photo Library:** CC Studio (cla). 26 **Mother & Baby Picture Library:** Ruth Jenkinson (bl) (cr). 27 **Science Photo Library:** Samuel Ashfield (b). 32 **SuperStock:** age fotostock (c). 33 **Getty Images:** Julia Smith (cr). 34 **Photolibrary:** Gyssels / BSIP Medical (br). **Science Photo Library:** Ian Hooton (bc). 37 **SuperStock:** Photononstop (bl). 44 **Alamy Images:** thislife pictures (c).

48 **Getty Images:** Marc Debnam (cr). 61 **Getty Images:** Roderick Chen (tl). 70 **Getty Images:** Bambu Productions (c); Rayes (bc). 73 **Mother & Baby Picture Library:** Paul Mitchell (tl). 77 **Mother & Baby Picture Library:** Ian Hooton (l). 79 **Mother & Baby Picture Library:** Ian Boddy (br). 95 **Dorling Kindersley:** Jamie Marshall (br). 98 **Alamy Images:** Paul Melling (br). 107 **Getty Images:** Tony Anderson (r). 109 **Mother & Baby Picture Library:** Ian Hooton (tr). 110 **Getty Images:** B2M Productions (br). 116 **Mother & Baby Picture Library:** Ian Hooton (cra) (bc) (br). 121 **Getty Images:** Bruce Ayres (tl); Zia Soleil (bc). 122 **Getty Images:** Chad Ehlers. 123 **Getty Images:** Paul Loven (tl). 124-125 **Getty Images:** Jose Luis Pelaez, Inc. 126 **Getty Images:** Frank Herholdt (bl). 127 **Corbis:** Larry Williams (r). 130 **iStockphoto.com:** Brian Powell. 131 **Getty Images:** Jupiterimages (tc); LWA (b). 132 **Corbis:** LWA-Sharie Kennedy (bc). 133 **Mother & Baby Picture Library:** Ian Hooton (b). 135 **Getty Images:** Noel Hendrickson (tl). 142 **Corbis:** Norbert Schaefer (c). 145 **Mother & Baby Picture Library:** Ian Hooton (tl). 152 **Getty Images:** Christa Renee (br). **Mother & Baby Picture Library:** Ian Hooton (bc). 165 **Getty Images:** Stefan Wettainen (br). 166-167 **Corbis:** Kevin Dodge. 168 **Getty Images:** Design Pics. 169 **Getty Images:** Philipe Cheng (b). 171 **Alamy Images:** Oredia (c). 172 **Corbis:** RCWW, Inc. (bl). **Getty Images:** Jim Jordan Photography (cr); Clarissa Leahy (c). 173 **Getty Images:** Martha Lazar. 176 **Getty Images:** B2M Productions (c). **Mother & Baby Picture Library:** Ian Hooton (bl). 177 **Photolibrary:** Jan Richter. 178 **Getty Images:** Cristian Baitg (c). 179 **Getty Images:** Stephen Chiang (tl). **iStockphoto.com:** Mark Goddard (tc). 180 **Getty Images:** Bill Sykes Images (ca); Photodisc (bl). 181 **Getty Images:** DK Stock/Nancy Ney (bl); Southern Stock (br). 182 **Alamy Images:** vario images GmbH & Co.KG (cr). **Mother & Baby Picture Library:** Paul Mitchell (br). **Photolibrary:** Antoine Dubroux (bc); Jan Richter (c). 183 **Photolibrary:** Pernille Tofte. 184 **Getty Images:** Stuart O'Sullivan (c). 185 **Getty Images:** Betsie Van Der Meer (tc). **Mother & Baby Picture Library:** Ian Hooton (tl). 186 **Getty Images:** David Hanover (br); Regine Mahaux (cr); David Oliver (bl). 187 **Getty Images:** Ghislain & Marie David de Lossy (br); Betsie Van Der Meer (l)

All other images © Dorling Kindersley
For further information see: www.dkimages.com